Richard Baker's Music Guide

Richard Baker's
Music Guide

With the help of a few familiar landmarks,
the well-known broadcaster invites you to discover
a wider world of pleasure in music.

DAVID & CHARLES
Newton Abbot London North Pomfret (Vt)

Illustrated by Evelyn Bartlett

British Library Cataloguing in Publication Data

Baker, Richard, b. 1925
   Your guide to good music.
   1. Music – Analysis, appreciation
   I. Title
   780'.15   MT6

   ISBN 0-7153-7782-5

Set by Trade Linotype Limited
and printed in Great Britain
by Redwood Burn Limited Trowbridge and Esher
for David & Charles (Publishers) Limited
Brunel House Newton Abbot Devon

Published in the United States of America
by David & Charles Inc
North Pomfret Vermont 05053 USA

CONTENTS

5

7

ACKNOWLEDGEMENTS

The author wishes to thank Miss Margaret Dowson for typing the manuscript of this book, and Mr Clive Bennett for reading it and making many useful suggestions.

PRELUDE

This book is intended as a guidebook and, since journeys without destinations are apt to be frustrating, let us begin by deciding where we intend to go.

First of all let me say that this book IS NOT for those who already know their way around the musical repertoire; IT IS for those who 'know what they like' and would like to know a bit more. As a result of my work on BBC Radio 4 record programmes over the years, I have had a great many letters from listeners, most of whom, I am glad to say, tell me that they enjoy them. But there is a minority – and I sympathise with their view – who do not want to hear anything they have not heard before; and there is another rather disheartening group who – again understandably – want to hear nothing unless it is by British composers and/or performed in English by British performers. Now I am second to none in my love of the music of these islands and my admiration for British musicians, but you cannot run a record programme for several years without venturing beyond our own shores and our own language, and stepping outside the limits imposed by universally known items in the repertoire – what might be called the 'classical top of the pops'. Fortunately a large proportion of listeners seem happy to explore a little further with me, so long as we do not stray too far from well-trodden paths. If that is how *you* feel about listening to music, this is the book for you.

I have arranged the text under such headings as Opera, Ballet Music, The Concerto, Symphonic Music and so on. In each section I have selected a number of compositions which come into the 'top of the pops' category – such as Bach's 'Air on the G String', Handel's 'Largo', the slow movement of Beethoven's 'Moonlight' Sonata, 'Nimrod' from Elgar's 'Enigma'

Variations – and then suggested in each case other music in a similar vein, which is less well known but just as attractive. I have not ventured at all into the realms of experimental music, important though it is; everything I have mentioned conforms to the admirable definition of good music attributed to the late Sir Thomas Beecham: 'Good music', he said, 'is that which penetrates the ear with facility and quits the memory with difficulty.'

Although I hope the book will steer more customers towards our concert halls and opera houses, I imagine that many readers will want to conduct their musical exploration with the aid of a gramophone. I have therefore included a few guidelines on the choice of records, though I strongly recommend those interested to consult such specialist magazines as *The Gramophone* or *Hi-Fi News*. There is also a short book list for those who want to read further; and in addition to my hundred or so top tunes and their derivatives, I have included sections devoted to musical humour and to a personal top twelve of my own choosing.

In fact the whole book is a personal one, and I am well aware that someone else would make other choices and other suggestions throughout. Here, quite simply, are a few pointers I have followed and found useful. I hope that through them you too will come to enjoy a wider range of music.

1
THE PIANO

Algernon:	Did you hear what I was playing, Lane?
Lane:	I didn't think it polite to listen, Sir.
Algernon:	I'm sorry for that, for your sake. I don't play accurately -- anyone can play accurately -- but I play with wonderful expression.

Oscar Wilde, *The Importance of Being Earnest*

How surely that little exchange from Wilde's masterpiece strikes home with those who, like myself, play the piano chiefly to amuse themselves. There is an immense repertoire expressly composed for the piano – and almost everything that was not originally written for the most universal of instruments seems to have been arranged for it – but a good many amateur pianists are strangely unadventurous. Of course, they may be discouraged by the problem of sight-reading with tolerable fluency, but this can be overcome by practising on simple compositions, such as hymns, which come in a wide variety of keys and can be used to provide a progressive challenge.

There follow a few indications of the range of the piano repertoire, broadening out from ten popular favourites. This, it is hoped, may be helpful to budding pianists and lovers of recorded piano music alike.

MOZART : 'RONDO ALLA TURCA' (TURKISH RONDO) FROM SONATA IN A (K 331)

In choosing a familiar example from Mozart's large output of keyboard music I hovered between this essay in the Turkish style, which was thought exotic in the eighteenth century, and the first movement of another Mozart sonata, in C major (K 545). By the way, in case you weren't sure, the 'K' stands for Ludwig von Köchel (1800–77), a botanist and mineralogist who was familiar with the principles of scientific classification and applied them usefully to the vast unsorted mass of Mozart's music; and the word 'sonata' is simply the Italian for a piece 'sounded' by instruments rather than sung ('cantata'). The first movement of the Sonata in C major got turned into a dainty little number that was very popular a generation ago, called 'In an Eighteenth-Century Drawing Room'. This presented an artificially pretty picture of the eighteenth century and a misleading view of Mozart who, in the same year (1788) that he produced this small-scale sonata for teaching purposes, also composed his three greatest symphonies, nos 39, 40 and 41, in the space of six weeks.

Although, like all the finest artists, he transcends historical barriers, Wolfgang Amadeus Mozart (1756–91) was also a man of his time – a time when musicians (the lucky ones) ranked as junior servants in the establishment of some great man; they had to make music to order, just as the cook had to come up with a good dinner, or else. In the second half of the eighteenth century, the pianoforte – or the forte-piano as it was often called in those days – was still in the process of taking over from the harpsichord as *the* domestic instrument. As a result it was fashionable to possess a piano, fashionable for the ladies to play it, and an immense demand for music for the new instrument was set up.

There was, of course, the legacy of such great keyboard com-

12

posers as Johann Sebastian Bach (1685–1750), whose forty-eight preludes and fugues have become a staple component of the piano repertoire, though they were not written specifically for it; and Domenico Scarlatti (1685–1757) who wrote well over five hundred short, brilliant keyboard sonatas. Muzio Clementi (1752–1832) is widely regarded as the first true pianoforte composer – he wrote numerous sonatas and a system of piano study – though the first known sonata for the 'soft-loud harpsichord, the one with hammers' dates from 1732. Mozart wrote nineteen keyboard sonatas and many other pieces which explore ever more deeply the possibilities of the piano; some of them are magnificent, like the great C minor Sonata (K 475) with its associated Fantasia (K 457). The keyboard output of Joseph Haydn (1732–1809) includes more than fifty sonatas. Two of J. S. Bach's sons produced a good deal of keyboard music : much of the work of Carl Philipp Emanuel Bach (1714–88) was thought advanced for his time, and he wrote a useful treatise called *The True Manner of Keyboard Performance*; Johann Christian Bach (1735–82) composed pieces for the harpsichord which, in the words of a contemporary diarist, 'ladies can execute with little trouble'.

Until the advent of Mozart with his sonatas and superb concertos for the piano, it was the brilliant, decorative abilities of the instrument which were chiefly exploited; but from then on, keeping step with progress in pianoforte construction, composers increasingly realised its expressive qualities.

BEETHOVEN : FIRST MOVEMENT, SONATA IN C SHARP MINOR
OP 27 NO 2 ('MOONLIGHT')

It was the critic Rellstab who said that the elegiac first movement of this 'Sonata Quasi una Fantasia' (sonata in the style of a fantasia) reminded him of moonlight on the Lake of Lucerne, thus bestowing one of music's most familiar nicknames. When the work was published in 1802, it was described as a sonata for harpsichord *or* pianoforte, though it is hard to imagine it played without the piano's capacity for sustained melody. Ludwig van Beethoven (1770–1827) made such heavy demands on his pianos that he broke several of them; he seems to have wanted them to do all the work of an orchestra and more. In the process he gave the world some of the greatest works ever composed for the instrument, among them the thirty-two piano sonatas. The slow movement of the Sonata in C minor op 13 – to which he himself gave the title 'Pathétique' – is almost as much loved as the first movement of the 'Moonlight'. It was a publisher who called the F minor Sonata, op 57, the 'Appassionata', reflecting its intense emotional quality, and another who dubbed op 28 in D the 'Pastoral'. By request, Beethoven himself gave a programme and a title to op 81a, 'Les Adieux . . .' (Farewell, Absence and Return); and op 106, perhaps the most titanic of all the sonatas, is known to us as the 'Hammerklavier', though as the word simply means 'pianoforte' in German, it could equally well apply to any piano composition. There is no Beethoven sonata, named or otherwise, which does not repay the attention of student or listener, for the series ranges from brisk cheerfulness to some of the most profound of all musical utterances.

Beethoven himself was a fine pianist, but he was not without rivals as a performer: among them the Hungarian Johann Nepomuk Hummel (1778–1837) who wrote an influential *Piano School* and was greatly admired for his brilliant technique and ability to improvise. One of Beethoven's pupils was Carl Czerny (1791–1857) who wrote nearly a thousand compositions, including hundreds for the piano. The studies in the three volumes of his *Complete Theoretical and Practical Pianoforte School* are still valuable to students and many of his other compositions deserve something better than oblivion.

The chief importance of Carl Maria von Weber (1786–1826) in musical history was as an operatic composer, but he was also a fine pianist and his works for piano solo and piano with orchestra have originality as well as brilliance. His *Invitation to the Dance* op 65 is a great piano favourite, and among the concerto-type works, the Konzertstück (Concert Piece) in F minor is well known and very attractive.

SCHUBERT : MOMENT MUSICAL IN F MINOR, OP 94 NO 3

Some music-lovers feel that the genius of Franz Schubert (1797–1828) found its supreme expression in short rather than extended

14

works. He composed some of the finest songs ever written, in which the piano often plays a part as important as that of the voice, and some beautiful pieces for piano solo. Schubert wrote a number of piano sonatas, all of which contain glorious music but are somewhat uneven in inspiration, and committed to paper a huge number of dances of all kinds, which must nevertheless be just a small proportion of the tunes he used to improvise for hours on end at the request of his friends. Among them are minuets, waltzes and écossaises – a form of dance, very popular at that period, which had nothing but its name to connect it with Scotland.

Of his six *Moments Musicaux* (Musical Moments), all of them pleasing, the most famous is the one in F minor. In a grander category altogether is the splendid Fantasy in C major op 15, known as 'The Wanderer' because its slow movement is based on Schubert's song of that name; and the eight Impromptus of op 90 and op 91 represent Schubert's piano writing at its magical best.

SCHUMANN : 'TRÄUMEREI' FROM SCENES OF CHILDHOOD OP 15

A major feature of the Romantic movement in music was that composers used their art to reflect and affect human emotions, to paint pictures and tell stories. Robert Schumann (1810–56) was the arch-Romantic in this and other respects; as a journalist he was among the intellectual leaders of the movement in Germany and he used music – as in the *Davidsbündlertänze* (Dances of the League of David) op 6 – as a weapon in the struggle against the Philistines of his own day. Schumann's overwhelming love for Clara Wieck, who became his wife only after a long struggle in the face of her father's opposition, was the direct inspiration of much of his music, which reflects a poet's awareness of the world.

'Träumerei' (Dreaming) is one of thirteen short pieces, most of which tell stories, included in the collection called *Kinderscenen* (Scenes of Childhood) op 15. Some fifty little compositions designed for young fingers to play make up the *Album for the Young*. But Schumann's piano music is rarely easy and some of it makes great technical demands. *Carnaval* op 9, with its

15

miniature portraits of characters from the *commedia dell'arte* such as Pierrot and Columbine, together with creatures of Schumann's own fantasy, culminates in the 'March of the League of David', to which, in imagination, all the composer's friends, real and fictitious, belonged.

Other sets of piano pieces include *Papillons* (Butterflies) op 2, *Albumblätter* (Album Leaves) op 124, and *Waldscenen* (Woodland Scenes) op 82. On a grander scale are the Fantasy in C major op 17 – a magnificent work dedicated successively to two brilliant pianists, the beloved Clara and Franz Liszt; the 'fantasy pictures' of *Faschingsschwank aus Wien* (Carnival Jest from Vienna) op 26; and the eight Fantasies of *Kreisleriana* op 16. Schumann's Piano Concerto in A minor is one of the best, and best-loved, works in that genre.

Always finely balanced in his emotional make-up, Schumann suffered a mental breakdown in his last years and died when he was only forty-six. The best of his music expresses a young man's ardent intensity of feeling, and much of it was written for the piano, whether as a solo instrument or in partnership with a singer in the composer's hundreds of wonderful songs. In an age when the sentiments and sufferings of the individual were felt to be of supreme importance, the pianoforte, which by now had developed into an instrument of great power and range, was the perfect means of expressing them.

CHOPIN : FANTAISIE-IMPROMPTU OP 66

Of Frédéric Chopin (1810–49), Arthur Hedley wrote in his biography that 'he and his piano formed one being and to write perfectly for it was second nature to him'. The publication of Chopin's earliest works led to an oft-quoted salute from Schumann : 'Hats off, gentlemen, a genius !' and his unique style as a performer was acclaimed from his boyhood days in Poland. His father, French by birth, was Polish by adoption; although Paris eventually became the centre of Chopin's life, he was passionately attached to his native Poland and gave expression to his patriotic feelings in some of his finest works.

That acute observer Hector Berlioz described Chopin as 'strictly the virtuoso of the elegant salon, the intimate gathering'

16

and indeed it was in aristocratic society that the graceful young man felt most at home. The *Fantaisie-Impromptu*, like so many of Chopin's works, was intended for one of the society ladies who surrounded him, Madame d'Este, though it was not published until after the composer's death.

Just as familiar to the general public are the study [no 3] in E major op 10 no 3 – which was turned into a popular song under the title 'Tristesse' or 'So Deep is the Night' – and the so-called 'Raindrop' Prelude, no 15 in D Flat from the set of Preludes op 28.

Unconsciously perhaps, Chopin followed Liszt's maxim, 'When at court, keep it short', in the pieces which first brought him fame and success in Paris – the nocturnes, the waltzes, the twenty-four preludes – proving thereby that the length of a work is no criterion of its musical value. The two sets of Studies, op 10 and op 25, demonstrated that technical exercises could at the same time be adventurous and satisfying compositions.

Chopin's sixty mazurkas reflected his lifelong interest in Polish folk music, and the spirit of patriotism inspired the splendid polonaises – the ones in A major and A Flat are universally known. Of his works on a larger scale, the four ballades are also suffused with patriotic feeling; they rank with the four scherzos and the F minor Fantasy among his more extended contributions to the piano repertoire.

The would-be performer of Chopin's music faces many problems of technique and interpretation. How wayward, for example, can one be in the matter of rhythm? On the one hand there is the assertion of Berlioz that 'Chopin simply could not play in strict time'; on the other hand, he was thought of by his contemporaries as the successor to Mozart – and it was Chopin's request that Mozart's Requiem be played at his funeral. Bach was among the composers Chopin studied as a boy, and one of the finest twentieth-century interpreters of Chopin's music, the Romanian pianist Dinu Lipatti, was also a magnificent Bach player. An aristocratic brilliance and an aristocratic restraint are alike required in the performance of Chopin's romantic music.

Franz Liszt (1811–86) was influential in every aspect of European music, but it was as a piano virtuoso that he first came before the public at the age of nine and he developed into one of the world's most sensational pianists as well as a prolific composer for the instrument. The three *Liebesträume* (Dreams of Love) were based on song settings of romantic poems whose words were sometimes printed above the solo piano score; the third is one of the best-known piano pieces ever written. It is an example of the seductive melodies with which Franz Liszt was able to conquer countless female hearts, but it scarcely suggests the immense range of Liszt's achievements as a composer. Leaving aside the works he wrote for voices and other instruments, his compositions for piano are numbered in hundreds, from the early studies of 1827 to the late pieces which look forward harmonically to the future.

Liszt's piano output can be divided into original works and transcriptions of pieces by other composers; the latter were sometimes direct re-workings for piano of orchestral scores and songs – a process which in those days was a kind of substitute for the gramophone – and sometimes fantasies on, for example, operatic themes, which were in themselves works of some complexity and originality.

In a sense the nineteen *Hungarian Rhapsodies* – based on gypsy themes rather than strictly Hungarian folk tunes – come into this category; although no 2 deserves its universal fame, it should not be heard to the exclusion of the others. Among the best known of the very numerous operatic transcriptions are the *Rigoletto* paraphrase, based mainly on the quartet from Verdi's opera, and the very successful transcription of the waltz from Gounod's *Faust*. Liszt also helped greatly to publicise Wagner's music by transcribing many passages from his operas, impossible though that task would appear; he even managed to translate to the keyboard the soaring phrases and opulent orchestration of the final scene of *Tristan und Isolde*, the noble 'Liebestod' (Love Death). The *'Paganini' Studies* – including the famous 'La Campanella' (The Little Bell) – are virtuoso transcriptions for piano of five of Paganini's Caprices for solo violin and a movement of his Violin Concerto no 2.

18

Liszt's original works for the piano reflect the conflict in the composer's nature betwen satanic brilliance and profound sensitivity. On the one hand there are the *Transcendental Studies* ('Etudes d'éxécution transcendante'), which laid the foundation of modern piano technique, and on the other the poetic scenes evoked in the sets of pieces entitled *Years of Pilgrimage* which, recalling as they do various experiences of Liszt's travels, are a kind of musical Cook's tour of the Europe of his day. In the undemanding manner of the *Liebesträume* are the six *Consolations* written for the Grand Duchess Anna Pavlovna and published in 1850; in contrast there is the magnificent complexity of Liszt's single piano sonata (in B minor) written just two years later. With his immense talent and generosity of spirit Liszt bequeathed to the world a great deal more than sentiment and sensation.

MENDELSSOHN : 'SPRING SONG' FROM OP 62

In all, Felix Mendelssohn (1809–47) wrote eight books of *Songs without Words* – short melodious pieces which, in the words of *Grove's Dictionary of Music*, were never intended to be more than 'affectionate contributions to autograph albums'. None of them is more than moderately difficult to play and they contributed greatly to Mendelssohn's popularity as a 'drawing-room composer'. The charming piece in A major known as 'Spring Song', from the fifth book of *Songs without Words*, was originally called 'Camberwell Green'; it was composed in a house whose site is now marked by a sundial in Ruskin Park, Camberwell, in south-east London. 'The Bee's Wedding' comes from the sixth book of the set, and is known in German as 'Spinnerlied' (Spinning Song); neither title is authentic, though Mendelssohn *did* bestow the names 'Duetto', 'Gondola Song', and 'Folk Song' on some familiar *Songs without Words*. Of his other compositions for solo piano, the Rondo Capriccioso in E major of op 14 is particularly well known and brilliant.

The demand for relatively easy pieces for the drawing-room piano grew apace during the nineteenth century; prominent among the composers who satisfied this need with music of real quality was Edvard Grieg (1843–1907). Brought up on the music of Mozart, Weber and Chopin, he was also influenced strongly by Schumann and subsequently by the folk music of his native Norway – influences which are clearly reflected in much of his music for solo piano. Grieg's Sonata in E minor op 7 is a fresh, vigorous work but he is best known to amateur pianists for his ten books of *Lyric Pieces*. The famous *Holberg Suite*, more familiar in Grieg's arrangement for string orchestra, was originally written for piano.

Grieg's compatriot Christian Sinding (1856–1941) wrote a great quantity of music, now largely forgotten with the exception of a single piano piece, *The Rustle of Spring* op 23 no 3, which seems to have been universally attempted by pianists of an earlier generation. Also remembered mainly for one piano piece, *Autumn* – though her flute music is also being heard again nowadays – is the French composer Cécile Chaminade (1857–1944). Dr Percy Scholes, in *The Oxford Companion to Music*, refers to her as 'the writer of tuneful and graceful short piano compositions with no intricacy of texture, no elaboration of form and no depth of feeling, but pleasant to hear and to play, and so tasteful in conception and execution as to disarm the highbrow critic'.

BRAHMS : WALTZ IN A FLAT FROM OP 39

The enchanting Waltz in A Flat, which I have chosen as a familiar example of the piano music of Johannes Brahms (1833–97), comes from the set of Waltzes op 39 originally written for pianoforte duet in 1865, not long after he had settled in the city of the waltz, Vienna. It is typical of the tender, lyrical strain of which Brahms was so exquisite a master.

Before the age of thirty, Brahms wrote two large-scale piano sonatas in C major and F Sharp minor, the very demanding and exciting *Variations on a Theme by Handel* op 24, as well as two sets of *Variations on a Theme of Paganini* op 35, and the rather less taxing Four Ballades of op 10 – one of them based on the Scottish ballad 'Edward', hence the generic title. There was then a gap of some fifteen years before Brahms again turned to writing for solo piano. In 1878–9 he wrote the eight pieces of op 76, including the well-known Capriccios in C major and B minor, and the Two Rhapsodies, op 79. Another long interval ensued before the final group of piano pieces, op 116–19, which include some of the most poetic compositions ever written for the piano, among them the fine E Flat major Intermezzo from op 117 and the great Rhapsody in E Flat from op 119. Brahms, unlike a great many composers of the Romantic period, did not believe in attaching descriptive titles to his music; in that respect, as in others, he belonged to the classical tradition, though he lacks nothing in Romantic fervour. The development of pianoforte music, with a growing freedom from classical forms, created the need for a new range of names for abstract pieces. Those which emerged included 'Nocturne', originated by the Irish pianist and composer John Field (1782–1837) and borrowed by Chopin; 'Ballade', first used by Chopin and inherited by Brahms among others; 'Intermezzo', for a small-scale composition; 'Rhapsody', for something grander in feeling and scale; and 'Capriccio', to describe a piece with a whimsical or humorous element. Brahms used them all, with others, to describe music which, at its best, is an intimate communion between composer and listener.

DEBUSSY : 'CLAIR DE LUNE'

Claude Achille Debussy (1862–1918) paralleled in music the ideas of contemporary artists and poets who were more interested in suggestion, in the play of light and colour, than in explicit statement. The famous 'Clair de Lune' (Moonlight), from the *Suite Bergamasque* of 1892, typifies this approach, with its muted chords and silvery nocturnal atmosphere. Debussy made much use of the pedals in his piano music and demanded a quite new refinement of style; the technique called for is elaborated in the two sets of his *Twelve Studies*. But it is poetry rather than technical display which distinguishes Debussy's many wonderful piano compositions. Book One of his *Préludes* includes such atmospheric masterpieces as 'La Fille aux Cheveux de Lin' (The Girl with the Flaxen Hair) and 'La Cathédrale Engloutie' (The Submerged Cathedral); in Book Two are the amusing 'Homage to S. Pickwick, Esq.' and 'Feux d'Artifice' (Fireworks). The suite *Children's Corner* contains an enchanting piece called 'The Snow is Dancing' as well as the well-known 'Golliwog's Cake Walk';

21

the evocative 'Soirée dans Grenade' (Evening in Granada) and 'Jardins sous la Pluie' (Gardens in the Rain) come from the three *Estampes* (Impressions) of 1903; and there are the two sets of *Images*, six beautiful pieces, among them 'Poissons d'Or' (Goldfish) and 'Reflets dans L'Eau' (Reflections in the Water). The two well-known *Arabesques* date from 1888, before Debussy had fully formed his own distinctive style.

Debussy belongs to a line of distinguished French pianist-composers which included in the previous generation Camille Saint-Säens (1835–1921) and Gabriel Fauré (1845–1924). Fauré wrote a good deal of piano music under such titles as 'Romance', 'Nocturne' and 'Barcarolle'; the Impromptu in F minor op 31 no 2 is a well-known example of his delicate, perfectly poised style. One of Fauré's pupils was Maurice Ravel (1875–1937), an accomplished pianist whose works for piano are distinguished though not very numerous. They include the Sonatina of 1905; the five pieces of *Miroirs* (Mirrors), among them the famous 'Alborada del Gracioso' (Morning Song of the Buffoon); the incredibly difficult *Gaspard de la Nuit* – three evocations of ghostly, sinister scenes – and *Le Tombeau de Couperin* (The Tomb of Couperin), a set of six pieces demonstrating Ravel's interest in music of an earlier age. This interest is also expressed in the well-known *Pavane pour une Infante Défunte* of 1899; it may be translated as 'Pavane for a Dead Infanta', but that does not do justice to the French title which Ravel chose, in the Impressionist manner, for its sound rather than its sense – it had no direct bearing on the death of a Spanish princess, though Ravel, like a number of other French composers, was greatly interested in the music of Spain.

At about this time Spain produced two remarkable pianist-composers in Isaac Albéniz (1860–1909) and Enrique Granados (1867–1916). Among many other piano pieces, Albéniz wrote a tango which used to be widely performed, but his major work for the instrument was *Ibéria*; dating from the years 1906–9, it consists of twelve pieces based on the various districts and dance rhythms of Spain. Granados too was greatly influenced by Spanish folk music – in his *Goyescas*, for example, and in the less elaborate *Spanish Dances*, of which there are four sets.

22

Sergei Rachmaninoff (1873–1943) wrote his famous – or infamous – Prelude in C Sharp minor in 1892 when he was only nineteen, and lived to regret it. Wherever he performed, during his career as one of the greatest of piano virtuosi, his audiences would not let him leave the platform without playing it. This Prelude, for all its over-exposure, is a highly effective romantic essay full of the sound of bells, which indeed is to be heard in much of Rachmaninoff's music. The C Sharp minor does not belong to his two sets of Preludes, op 23 and 32, though these contain many fine compositions; among the most effective are op 23 no 5 in G minor and op 32 no 10 in B minor. The two sets of *Etudes-Tableaux* (Study Pictures), op 33 and 39, also illustrate the composer's brilliance and his gift for nostalgic melody. Rachmaninoff's piano music is very satisfying to listen to; as for playing it – only high-grade pianists need apply.

The Hungarian pianist and composer Ernö Dohnanyi (1877–1960), a musician somewhat in the Rachmaninoff manner, wrote a good many pieces for the piano. As a soloist of great brilliance, he believed in living dangerously himself and expected his interpreters to do likewise; even such a well-tried favourite as the Rhapsody no 3 in C major presents considerable technical difficulties.

Dohnanyi was a powerful early influence on two other Hungarian composers – Béla Bartók (1881–1945) and Zoltan Kodály (1882–1967). Bartók in particular had a great feeling for the piano and derived most of his hard-won income from playing and giving pianoforte lessons; as a composer he reacted against the romantic concept of the instrument and began exploiting its percussive aspects. Between 1926 and 1937, Bartók developed his ideas on piano technique in the six volumes of *Mikrokosmos* (Microcosm) – 153 pieces in all, graded from very simple to very difficult.

Many other notable twentieth-century composers have written for the piano: the Russian Serge Prokofiev (1891–1953), with his very considerable output of sweet-and-sour music for the instrument, including eight fine sonatas; Francis Poulenc (1899–1963), who composed a number of diverting piano pieces apart from the often-heard *Mouvement Perpetuel* of 1918; and, among British composers, Arnold Bax (1883–1953) and John Ireland (1879–1962). Ireland's many delightful piano pieces are fortunately arousing renewed interest.

When we consider the music of very recent times we are driven to ask 'Whatever happened to the piano?' Less and less music seems to be written for it as a solo instrument. This decline parallels the growth of radio, television and the gramophone as the principal media of home entertainment; for some, perhaps, the piano symbolises too strongly a past age of romantic grandeur and middle-class affluence.

For whatever reason, contemporary composers seem in general to have lost interest in the piano, except as a percussion instrument, sometimes made to sound in ways never thought of by its inventors. There is, however, a renewed enthusiasm for the piano's ancestors, and early forms of the instrument – the 'square piano' and 'forte-piano' of Mozart's and Beethoven's day – have been refurbished and imitated by modern makers to provide a more 'authentic' sound. Could it be that the grand piano in its turn is doomed to extinction, to be revived a couple of centuries hence by musical antiquarians?

2
OTHER SOLO INSTRUMENTS

VIOLIN — FIOCCO : ALLEGRO

'Tis God gives skill,
But not without men's hands :
he could not make Antonio Stradivari's violins
Without Antonio.

George Eliot, 'Stradivarius'

Joseph-Hector Fiocco (1703–41) was born and died in Belgium, although his family was of Italian origin. He made violins as well as writing music for them, and was one of those thoroughly worthy musicians who are known to posterity through a single composition; his *Allegro*, which is a familiar set piece for students of the violin, is chosen here as an example of the vast quantity of classical and pre-classical music written for the instrument.

The violin first appeared on the musical scene in the early sixteenth century, perhaps in Poland, but soon became specially popular in Italy, where two great schools of violin-making were established at Brescia and Cremona. At Cremona, Nicolo Amati (1596–1684) was succeeded by the greatest master of all, Antonio Stradivari (c 1644–1737), and by Giuseppe Guarneri (1698–1744). The creation of beautiful instruments was paralleled by an outpouring of fine music for violins and the other instruments of the violin family by such composer-performers as Antonio Vivaldi (1678–1741), Arcangelo Corelli (1653–1713), and Giuseppe Tartini (1692–1770), acclaimed virtuoso and composer of the well-known 'Devil's Trill' Sonata. Although the string family today is confined to violin, viola, cello and double-bass, in those days it included the viola d'amore, viola da gamba, viola pomposa, cello piccolo, violino piccolo and several others, all of which had concertos or solos written for them.

Skilful though these early violin composers were, their works present no great technical problems to the good modern violinist – though it must be said that one composer of the period, Johann Sebastian Bach, in his sonatas and partitas for violin (which include the well-known *Chaconne*), still offers a formidable challenge to the virtuoso.

VIOLIN – PAGANINI : CAPRICE IN A MINOR

From this did Paganini comb the fierce
Electric sparks, or to tenuity
Pull forth the inmost wailing of the wire –
No cat-gut could swoon out so much of soul.

Robert Browning, 'Red Cotton Nightcap Country'

The idea of the Devil as a fiddler is a very ancient one; it was his appearance in this guise to the dreaming Tartini which is said to have inspired the 'Devil's Trill' Sonata, and in 1734 Guarneri made a fine instrument which became known as 'the Devil's violin'. Browning's poem, quoted above, refers to

The Devil, that old stager . . . who leads
Downward, perhaps, but fiddles all the way

and to the widely prevalent notion that Niccolò Paganini (1782–1840) could only play as he did because he was in league with the Devil.

Paganini did little to discourage this belief: it was good for publicity and helped to make him one of the greatest musical celebrities of his day. He was in fact a superlative player who studied the early masters closely, but went far beyond them in exploring the technical possibilities of the violin. He was a source of inspiration to other musicians in many respects; the Caprice in A minor, from his twenty-four Caprices for unaccompanied violin, was adopted by several other composers, among them Rachmaninoff who used it as the basis for his *Rhapsody on a Theme of Paganini* for piano and orchestra. Paganini has also gone down in history as a man of great generosity, chiefly on account of the gift of money he made to Berlioz at a bad moment in that composer's career. However, having asked Berlioz to write him a concerto for the violin's larger brother the viola, he lost interest when the composer produced a symphonic work, *Harold in Italy*, in which the soloist was required to be silent at times! (The viola did not really come into its own as a solo instrument until the British player Lionel Tertis (1876–1975) showed what it could do and the composer Paul Hindemith (1895–1963) also became a viola virtuoso.)

Paganini's fantastic virtuosity was emulated later in the nineteenth century by a number of other remarkable performers, among them the Belgian Henri Vieuxtemps (1820–81), the Spaniard Pablo de Sarasate (1844–1908), Henri Wieniawski, who was born in Poland in 1835 and died in Moscow in 1880, and Joseph Joachim (1831–1907). All composed extensively for the violin as well as being master performers. The tradition was inherited by Fritz Kreisler (1875–1962), who wrote a number of attractive compositions under his own name, such as the *Caprice Viennois*, inspired by his native city of Vienna; he also created, with quite fictitious attributions, a number of works in the style of earlier masters, among them *Pugnani's Praeludium and Allegro* and *Tartini's Variations on a Theme by Corelli*.

Monsieur, vous me faites croire aux miracles : vous savez faire d'un boeuf un rossignol !
(Sir, you make me believe in miracles; you know how to turn an ox into a nightingale !)

Voltaire, to the cellist Duport

In 1907 the choreographer Fokine used this music for a ballet, *The Dying Swan*, designed for the great Anna Pavlova, and thus reinforced the image of the violoncello as the most soulful of instruments. The cello owes its popularity as a solo instrument in our time – and to some extent its repertoire – to one great performer, the Catalan Pablo Casals (1875–1973). Exiled from Spain by the Franco government after the Spanish civil war, Casals spent the rest of his life in the small French Pyrenean village of Prades, which became a place of pilgrimage for all who admired his artistry and his political courage.

Casals' repertoire was rooted in the six suites for unaccompanied cello by Bach, whose music became, in his hands, a spiritual experience; he revived interest in the cello concertos of Haydn, Schumann, Dvořák and others, and stimulated a number of twentieth-century composers to write for the instrument. Among classical sonatas for cello and piano, the five of Beethoven and the two written by Brahms are outstanding.

More recently, the great Russian cellist Mstislav Rostropovich, among other notable performers, has done much to enhance the status of the cello. At the height of his playing career (he is now turning more and more to conducting) he appeared in London in a series of concerts comprising no fewer than thirty-one works for cello and orchestra; and his friendship with Benjamin Britten (1913–76) led to a number of fine works for the instrument, including the remarkable Cello Symphony.

In earlier days the cello took longer than the violin to establish itself in public favour, but its place was assured when the string quartet settled into its present form (two violins, viola and cello) in the days of Haydn and Mozart. Among lighter compositions for the cello, those of the virtuoso David Popper (1843–1913) are attractive, and one of the instrument's most popular annual appearances must surely be in Sir Henry Wood's *Fantasia on British Sea Songs* at the Last Night of the Proms, when the principal cellist takes the solo in 'Tom Bowling'.

The double-bass, grandfather – and sometimes buffoon – of the violin family, also has its solo repertoire; among its virtuosi have been Dragonetti, a contemporary of Rossini, and Serge Koussevitsky, better known for his period as conductor of the Boston Symphony Orchestra.

GUITAR – TARREGA : MEMORIES OF THE ALHAMBRA (TREMOLO STUDY)

The Owl looked up to the stars above
And sang to a small guitar,
'O lovely pussy, O pussy my love,
What a beautiful pussy you are!'

Edward Lear, 'The Owl and the Pussy-cat'

The guitar, whose name can be traced back to the Greek word *kithara*, was one of the most widely known and popular instruments long before, in its electronic mutations, it became indispensable to 'pop' music. As Edward Lear's Owl wisely knew, it is perfect as an accompanying instrument, in which role it is essential to the folk singer – but it is also, in the hands of a virtuoso, a solo instrument of great flexibility.

Music has been specially composed for the guitar, and its Spanish predecessor the *vihuela*, since the Middle Ages; towards the end of the eighteenth century the guitar began to be fashionable throughout musical Europe, aided by the compositions of Fernando Sor (1778–1839), who has been called 'the Beethoven of the guitar', and his Italian contemporary Mauro Giuliani (1781–1828). Schubert and Weber are known to have played the instrument; Paganini abandoned the violin for three years in favour of a guitar, which was later owned by Berlioz.

The history of the modern guitar really begins with Francisco Tarrega, who was born in Villareal in 1852 and died in Barcelona in 1909; the Tremolo Study, combining lyrical beauty with

29

technical problems, is perhaps his best-known piece, but it was Tarrega's skill in transcribing other people's music for the guitar which did so much to establish it as a major solo instrument. This in turn stimulated composers to write original music for it, so that the guitar now has a considerable repertoire of solo works and concertos. In 1893, during Tarrega's lifetime, another great guitarist was born; this was Andres Segovia, whose influence on the present generation of guitarists, among them Julian Bream and John Williams, is incalculable. He has also been a lifelong source of inspiration to composers.

Perhaps the best-loved guitar concerto is the *Concierto de Aranjuez*, written in 1939 by Joaquin Rodrigo, with its delicate scoring and magical slow movement. Of the vast quantity of music written for solo guitar, the preludes and studies of the Brazilian Heitor Villa-Lobos (1887–1959) are well known and attractive; and there are many works by Spanish composers, such as Albéniz, Granados and de Falla, which sound as though they were made for the guitar, even if originally they were not. Thanks to a succession of great players the guitar has become one of the most important instruments of the twentieth century.

ORGAN – BACH : TOCCATA AND FUGUE IN D MINOR

If an organist is master of his instrument, I rank
him among the first of virtuosi.

Beethoven, in a letter to Freudenberg

The organist has at his fingertips a larger and more varied repertoire than any other musician, except the pianist, and it is odd that so little of it is known to the general public. There are, of course, a great many well-informed organ enthusiasts, but they seem to form a separate sub-division of the 'music-lover' species, having little or no contact with the commoner kind. The location of many of the best instruments in places of worship rather than of entertainment may have something to do with the condition of 'apartheid' suffered by the organ in musical appreciation; magnificent though church organs often are, they somehow came to be imbued with the depressing legacy of the Victorian Sunday.

It was the large, often heavy sound of the nineteenth-century organ that the famous Promenade Concert conductor Sir Henry Wood (1869–1944) must have had in mind when he transcribed for symphony orchestra the splendid Toccata and Fugue in D minor of Johann Sebastian Bach (1685–1750). (Incidentally Wood, as an arranger, adopted the pseudonym Paul Klenovsky, which means in Russian 'one of the family of the Maple tree' – an apt choice, as well as being a dig at those critics who refused to take seriously any musician who could not boast a foreign name.) The Toccata and Fugue in orchestral form became even more famous through the Walt Disney/Leopold Stokowski film *Fantasia*.

In the last twenty-five years, fortunately, the heavy layers of varnish so often applied by conductors and arrangers to masterpieces of earlier days have been removed, and we are now able to appreciate the works of Bach, Handel and others more nearly as their composers intended. There has been a great revival of interest in organs of the seventeenth and eighteenth centuries; many instruments have been expertly restored, and new organs have been designed to reproduce the sound of the so-called Baroque period – a sound which is altogether clearer, cleaner and lighter in tone than that of the great nineteenth-century organ. It is a revelation to hear the Toccata and Fugue in D minor played on an organ in Hamburg which Bach himself may have used; recordings now exist of this and many other organ works by Bach played on contemporary instruments, and we can form a more authentic picture of the greatest organ composer who ever lived.

Bach had a brilliant facility for improvisation; probably only a small proportion of the music he created ever found its way on to manuscript paper. Of the organ preludes and fugues which have come down to us – they would probably have been lost for ever had it not been for the rediscovery of Bach by Mendelssohn – some have nicknames which have helped to make them specially well known; among these are 'St Anne's Fugue' in E Flat, the 'Wedge' Fugue in E minor, and the 'Jig' Fugue in G major. Bach's works are catalogued by numbers, with the prefix BWV (Bach Werke-Verzeichnis) – the index compiled by the musicologist Wolfgang Schmieder (b 1901).

Other important names in Baroque organ music are the

Danish Diderik Buxtehude (1637–1707), who influenced both Bach and Handel, and Johann Pachelbel (1653–1706), who taught Johann Christian Bach, the great Bach's elder brother.

ORGAN – WIDOR : TOCCATA FROM SYMPHONY NO 5

. . . it may be that only in Heaven
I shall hear that grand Amen.

Adelaide Ann Proctor (1825–64), 'The Lost Chord'

Since we are now discussing another toccata, it may be as well to explain that this Italian word simply means 'touched' (by the player's fingers); it is usually applied to a display piece, and the Toccata from the fifth symphony of Charles Marie Widor (1844–1937) is certainly that. Always a great favourite with organists, it acquired a new dimension of fame when it was played at the wedding of Princess Anne at Westminster Abbey in 1973. Widor wrote ten organ symphonies in all, as well as a large amount of other music, and belonged to a flourishing group of French and Belgian organ composers which also included César Franck (1822–90), Camille Saint-Saëns (1835–1921), Alexandre Guilmant (1837–1911) and Louis Vierne (1870–1937).

A work of this period which now almost rivals the Widor Toccata in popularity is the third symphony of Saint-Saëns for organ and orchestra, which demonstrates very well the rhetorical splendour of the French nineteenth-century school. Another exponent of the style was Louis James Alfred Léfébure-Wély (1817–79), a prodigy much admired in his own day but who was told frankly by Rossini that he was better loved for his faults than his virtues as a composer. Percy Scholes, compiling his *Oxford Companion to Music* in 1938, suggested that had Léfébure-Wély been living at that time he would have been entitled to 'the world's highest salary as a cinema organist'.

Works on such a grand scale – precursors of the immense compositions of Olivier Messiaen (b 1908) – would not have been possible without the skill of some remarkable organ builders who greatly enlarged the scope of the instrument at that period. In France the outstanding figure was Aristide Cavaillé-Coll (1811–

99). In Britain, Henry Willis (1821–1901) rebuilt half the cathedral organs in the country as well as constructing many very large concert-hall instruments, including the ones at the Royal Albert Hall and Alexandra Palace – the latter, alas, no longer playable – in London. In North America the construction of pipe organs, by such makers as Roosevelt in the USA and Cassavant in Canada, proceeded apace.

HARPSICHORD – DAQUIN : LE COUCOU

I went to hear Mrs. Turner's daughter play on the Harpsichon, but, Lord! it was enough to make any man sick to hear her; yet I was forced to commend her highly.

Samuel Pepys, Diary, 1 May 1663

There is a whole family of keyboard instruments whose strings, instead of being hit by a hammer, as in the pianoforte, are plucked by a quill. The small rectangular virginals of Elizabethan times, for which such masters as William Byrd (c 1543–1623), Giles Farnaby (c 1565–1640) and Orlando Gibbons (1583–1625) wrote fine music, was followed in the seventeenth and eighteenth centuries by the triangular spinet. The harpsichord – the first known example was made in Rome in 1521 – was from the outset designed on a much larger scale, with several strings to each note, and mechanical methods of varying the volume and tone; in external appearance it resembles a grand piano, except that many harpsichords have two manuals. Reaching a position of widespread importance in the seventeenth and eighteenth centuries, the harpsichord's popularity declined as the piano came on to the scene. Fortunately, though, the great revival of interest in pre-Romantic music in our times has led to a new life for the harpsichord; there are a number of modern makers of the instrument, which is now often heard in works of earlier days, as well as in new compositions of many kinds including 'pop'.

The Cuckoo by Louis Claude Daquin (1694–1772) is a short descriptive piece of a kind that was very fashionable in the France of Daquin's day; publishers of a later period might have

33

described it as a 'novelty item'. Daquin was a prodigy who, at the age of six, played the harpsichord before Louis XIV; he was one of a number of remarkable French keyboard composers of the period. François Couperin (1668–1733) wrote a treatise on harpsichord playing (*L'Art de toucher le Claveçin*) and a large number of keyboard pieces with descriptive titles; Jean Philippe Rameau (1683–1764) was another prolific composer for the harpsichord, as well as for the operatic stage. Bach and Handel both wrote a large amount of keyboard music, including a good many dances. Six harpsichords were specially made for Bach to his own specification : they were to have double keyboards and other refinements which would permit the performance of such complex works as his brilliant 'Italian Concerto'. Born in the same year as Bach and Handel, Domenico Scarlatti (1685–1757) wrote hundreds of ingenious and attractive harpsichord sonatas which may have been composed for an instrument with a single keyboard.

A great many records of harpsichord music are currently available. Among modern virtuosi, George Malcolm is among the most entertaining and versatile; he possesses in high degree the traditional keyboard performer's ability to improvise, and apart from his 'straight' performances has recorded some delightful lighter pieces such as Alec Templeton's *Bach goes to Town* and Rimsky-Korsakov's *The Flight of the Bumble Bee*.

FLUTE – GLUCK : 'DANCE OF THE BLESSED SPIRITS' FROM ORPHEUS AND EURYDICE

The Flute is an instrument of a strongly exciting, rather than of an ethical character, and should consequently be employed only upon occasions when the object is the purging of the emotions rather than the improvement of the mind.

Aristotle, *Politics*, Book VIII

The flute has been one of the most popular instruments since ancient times, and Shakespeare may well have been right when, in *Antony and Cleopatra*, he described the oars of Cleopatra's barge as keeping stroke to the tune of flutes; he was also thinking

of the amorous associations which traditionally belong to the
flute. In our own day the instrument has gained prominence for
the general public thanks to the skill and ebullient personality
of the Irish flautist James Galway. (At which point I pause and
reflect that Arthur Jacobs, in his *New Penguin Dictionary of
Music*, insists that the word 'flautist' is an Italianate Victorian
affectation, and that a flute player is more properly described in
English as a 'flutist'.)

'The Dance of the Blessed Spirits' is one of the most famous
of flute solos, expressing to perfection the serenity of the Elysian
Fields where, according to classical legend, the souls of the
virtuous find rest. Bach and Handel both wrote extensively for
the flute; so did Haydn. Mozart did not much like it as a solo
instrument but wrote for it all the same when commissioned to
do so; his Flute and Harp Concerto is a particularly enchanting
work. In the Victorian period, flute and harp were often heard
in consort, for the flute was considered the gentleman's instrument par excellence, while the harp was thought to provide a
lady with the perfect means of displaying a well-shaped pair of
arms.

Vast amounts of music for the flute appeared in the nineteenth
century, some of the most attractive by Benjamin Godard (1849–
95), Albert Doppler (1831–83) and his brother Karl (1825–1900),
and Cécile Chaminade (1857–1944). Numerous too were spectacular duets for soprano and flute obbligato, ranging from the
Mad Scene in the opera *Lucia di Lammermoor* by Gaetano
Donizetti (1797–1848) to such drawing-room display pieces as
'Lo, Here the Gentle Lark' by Sir Henry Bishop (1786–1855)
and 'The Gipsy and the Bird' by Sir Julius Benedict (1804–85).
These compositions exploit the agility of the flute to an almost
ludicrous extent, and it is fortunate that such composers as
Debussy – in his haunting short solo work *Syrinx* – and Ravel
have helped to explore once again the instrument's capacity for
poetic feeling.

OBOE – MOZART : OBOE QUARTET

With my wife to the King's House to see 'The Virgin
Martyr' . . . that which did please me beyond anything in

35

the whole world was the wind-music when the angel comes down, which is so sweet that it ravished me . . . and makes me resolve to practise wind-music, and to make my wife do the like.

Samuel Pepys, *Diary*, 27 February 1668

Although the other members of the woodwind family have been somewhat overshadowed in solo work by that prima donna, the flute, nevertheless the clarinet and the oboe, with its various relations, each has a considerable repertoire as a solo instrument, as well as in chamber music.

Clarinets appeared relatively recently on the musical scene; they were in use in the mid-eighteenth century, but as late as 1778, writing home to Salzburg from Mannheim, where there was a famous orchestra, Mozart could exclaim : 'If only we had clarinets! You can't guess the lordly effect of a symphony with flutes, oboes and clarinets.' Mozart loved the clarinet; he wrote a lovely quintet and concerto for the instrument, as well as using it in many other works. Weber (1786–1826) produced several very attractive compositions for it, including a very brilliant Grand Duo with accompanying piano, and Brahms wrote several beautiful chamber music works for the clarinet.

A sudden flowering of interest in any particular instrument always seems to stem from the talent of an outstanding performer : Mozart, Weber and Brahms were each stimulated to write for the clarinet through their acquaintance with a great player (Anton Stadler, H. J. Bärmann and Richard Mühlfeld respectively). In our days, mention of the oboe at once conjures up the name of Léon Goossens (b 1897), who has inspired a number of composers to write works for him or to adapt existing music for the oboe.

Unlike the clarinet, the oboe, with its double reed and conical-shaped tube, can trace its origins back to Roman times. The penetrating voices of this instrument and of its close relative, the bassoon, meant that in earlier times they were chiefly used in military music. Handel was fond of the oboe (or 'hautbois', as it was then called); there is a beautiful oboe solo in the 'Sinfonia' of Bach's *Christmas Oratorio*, and Mozart's Oboe Quartet is a delightful little work. Many other composers have written solo and chamber music for the instrument, but it is probably best known for its part in orchestral music. Its plaintive tone is heard to great effect, for example, in Tchaikovsky's *Swan Lake* ballet music, while its cousin, the cor anglais (English horn) has a long, haunting solo in *The Swan of Tuonela* by Sibelius (1865–1957). The repertoire of the bassoon has been greatly enlarged in our times through the work of another virtuoso, Archie Camden (b 1888); although well aware of its comic possibilities, as in his memorable playing of the *Variations on 'Lucy Long'*, he has also stimulated composers to produce a number of serious works for the instrument.

TRUMPET – CLARKE : TRUMPET VOLUNTARY

Smith's idea of heaven is, eating pâtés de foie gras to the sound of trumpets.

The Rev Sidney Smith, quoted in Hesketh Pearson,
The Smith of Smiths, 1934

When the tomb of the Egyptian Pharaoh Tutankhamun (reigned 1358–1353 BC) was opened in 1923, trumpets – which can still be played – were found there. Indeed, the blare of trumpets echoes down the years from the very beginnings of human history. It is the martial, ceremonial instrument *par excellence*, and such is its arresting effect that, according to the scriptures, we can expect to be summoned to the Day of Judgement by the sound of the Last Trump.

Bach made brilliant use of high trumpets (so-called Bach Trumpets) in, for example, his second Brandenburg Concerto; there is a fine *obbligato* in 'The Trumpet shall Sound' from Handel's *Messiah*, and another in the aria 'Let the Bright Seraphim' from the same composer's *Samson*. Haydn wrote a trumpet concerto. The famous *Trumpet Voluntary* was ascribed for many years to Henry Purcell (*c* 1658–95), but is now known to be by Jeremiah Clarke (*c* 1670–1707). It was first published not as a trumpet solo but in *A choice Collection of Ayres for the Harpsichord or Spinet* (1700) as 'The Prince of Denmark's March' : the prince in question was Queen Anne's consort. The trumpet plays an important role in the symphony orchestra, and is also used to great effect in a number of works for smaller combinations, though by nature it is not really fitted to music of the intimate kind.

One of the earliest 'instruments' used by man was the horn of an animal; this, when sounded, proved an ideal means of summoning people from a distance and giving signals for various purposes. Its value in hunting was soon recognised, and from this evolved the sophisticated modern French horn, with its 11 feet of curled tubing. Probably the most famous composition for the instrument is one of Mozart's four horn concertos, made very popular in recent times by the great player Denis Brain (1921–57), whose father Aubrey was also a notable virtuoso. Apart from its large and effective role in the modern orchestra, the French horn also has a repertoire of solo and chamber music, its tone being less strident than that of the trumpet. The trio for horn, violin and piano by Brahms is very beautiful; Beethoven wrote several chamber music works which use it; there is a stunning concert piece for four horns by Schumann and two fine concertos by Richard Strauss. On the lighter side, to remind us of the French horn's straight ancestors, is the famous *Post-Horn Galop* of Koenig.

3

CHAMBER MUSIC

The house was perpetually alive to the cool fern-like patterns of a quartet.

Lawrence Durrell, *Justine*

If large-scale works can be compared to public speeches, with all their capacity to excite – and to bore – then music for a few performers, designed to be heard in an intimate setting, is like the conversation of friends – a source, at its best, of refreshment and delight.

The Australian-born pianist and composer Percy Grainger (1882–1961), eager to let a draught of fresh air into the mustier areas of music, insisted on the term 'room music' instead of chamber music, and that is really a far more acceptable description of one of the most attractive of all musical forms.

Chamber music, as we now understand the term – meaning conversational music for two or more instruments in which each participant plays a part of more or less equal importance – can be said to begin with Joseph Haydn (1732–1809). Before his time, in the seventeenth and early eighteenth centuries, a vast amount of small-scale music had indeed been composed, for various combinations of instruments – the numerous sonatas of Bach, Handel and Corelli at once come to mind – but almost all these works made use of the harpsichord as a 'continuo' or accompanying instrument. Such a composition, designed for performance in a room, would often be called 'sonata da camera' to distinguish it from 'sonata da chiesa', music to be played in church. Incidentally, a great deal is expected from the harpsichordist in this kind of music, for generally he has to improvise the accompaniment on the basis of harmonic indications – a 'figured bass' – provided for him by the composer.

HAYDN : THEME AND VARIATIONS, QUARTET IN C OP 76 NO 3 ('EMPEROR')

Haydn was the first to bring to perfection the string quartet – for many people the most satisfying of all forms of music – employing two violins, a viola and cello. It may be that he first wrote for this combination of instruments simply because they happened to be available to him at the country house at Weinzierl where he stayed for some time in 1755. He created his first twelve string quartets for a group of musical friends there, and went on to compose eighty-three in all, as well as more than thirty piano trios – for piano, violin and cello – and a great deal of other chamber music.

One of the most famous pieces of quartet music ever written occurs in Haydn's Quartet op 76 no 3; it is called the 'Emperor' Quartet because the slow movement is based on the tune Haydn wrote – derived from an old Croatian melody – in 1797 as an Austrian national anthem, which is known to us as the hymn tune 'Austria' and, through its adoption by the Germans, as 'Deutschland über Alles'. Haydn loved the tune, as well he might; it is said to have been the last music he played before his death, which occurred in Vienna while the city was being bombarded by the French.

Mozart declared that it was from Haydn that he learned how to compose string quartets; he wrote twenty-three in all, dedicating a set of six of them to Haydn. However, Mozart also composed a great deal of chamber music for combinations other than the string quartet, including the already-mentioned Oboe Quartet, for oboe and strings, and the Clarinet Quintet, for clarinet and string quartet. The Köchel catalogue of Mozart's works lists among other things, some forty violin and piano sonatas, seven string quintets, two piano quartets (piano, violin, viola, cello) and seventeen divertimenti (diversions) for various groups of wind and string instruments. The 'infinite variety' of charms attributed by Shakespeare to Cleopatra applies equally to Mozart's chamber music; it is, to those who know and love it, just as irresistible.

BEETHOVEN : PIANO TRIO IN B FLAT OP 97 ('ARCHDUKE')

A considerable number of well-known compositions have attracted nicknames – a few bestowed by composers, some suggested by the character of the music, and some, as in this case, derived from the patron to whom the work is dedicated. The Archduke Rudolph was one of several aristocrats who were both patrons and pupils of Beethoven; the B Flat Trio for piano, violin and cello was sent to him in 1811 with a request from the composer that it should be copied 'only inside your Palace, as otherwise one is never sure it will not be stolen'. Beethoven clearly knew the value of this wonderful work; it is full of marvellous tunes of instant appeal and admirably resolves the problem of balance which always exists with this grouping of instruments. The 'Archduke' is one of his ten piano trios.

Beethoven also wrote ten sonatas for violin and piano; nicknames have helped to make two of them specially well known : the 'Spring' Sonata in F op 24, perhaps so called on account of the cheerful freshness of the opening theme, and the 'Kreutzer' in A op 47, dedicated to the violinist and composer Rudolph Kreutzer (1766–1831). Among Beethoven's large output of chamber music the Septet in E Flat op 20, written for clarinet, horn, bassoon, violin, viola, cello and double-bass, is unusual as well as attractive; while the seventeen string quartets range from the six delightful works of op 18 to some of the most profound music ever written – for example, the Quartet in C Sharp minor op 131, and the last work Beethoven completed, the Quartet in

41

F op 135. The latter has a final movement based on the question and answer 'Muss es sein?' ('Must it be?') – 'Es muss sein!' ('It must be!'). This could be read as a deep statement of philosophical resignation from one who had suffered much; equally, as the pianist Paul Hamburger pointed out, it could express Beethoven's unwillingness to write the last movement – or to pay his laundry bill. There was a vein of stubborn humour in Beethoven even when his circumstances were at their most hostile.

SCHUBERT: QUINTET IN A MAJOR, D 667 ('TROUT')

Nowadays Schubert's works are frequently identified by 'D' numbers instead of opus numbers; these relate to the thematic catalogue of his works published by the musicologist Otto Deutsch in 1951. Here, however, is another case of a composition best known by its nickname.

The second of the five movements of the A major Quintet is a set of variations on Schubert's song 'The Trout' – and this idea was the starting point for one of the most engaging of all chamber music works. The suggestion came from a wealthy mining engineer, Sylvester Paumgartner, who played the cello. He lived in the town of Steyr in Upper Austria where, in the summer of 1819, Schubert spent a holiday with his friend Johann Vogl; they often took part in the informal concerts Paumgartner arranged in his music room, and it was natural that the visiting composer should be called on to supply a new work. The somewhat unusual combination of piano, violin, viola, cello and double-bass was probably dictated by the players available – a factor which has influenced the form of many a chamber music composition over the years, including Schubert's enchanting Octet in F (D 803), composed five years later for the amateur clarinettist Count von Troyer and using the same instruments as in Beethoven's Septet in E Flat, with the addition of a second violin.

Among Schubert's many chamber music works, a handful, like the 'Trout' Quintet, have become especially well loved. The Piano Trio in B Flat (D 898), one of his two piano trios, must certainly be mentioned, together with the Quartet in D minor

(D 810), known as 'Death and the Maiden' after another of Schubert's songs which forms the basis of the second movement. If 'Death and the Maiden' is one of the finest chamber music works in the classical repertoire, the String Quintet in C major (D 956), for string quartet plus a second cello, must surely be reckoned among the most memorable, chiefly on account of its profoundly moving central Adagio. Altogether lighter in weight, but no less Schubertian for that, are the sonatas (or sonatinas) for violin and piano – accessible, attractive pieces of the kind Schubert produced with such copious generosity for his musical friends.

TCHAIKOVSKY : ANDANTE CANTABILE, STRING QUARTET IN D OP 11

In the hands of Schubert and Beethoven the string quartet, like other musical forms, became to some extent a medium for the expression of personal feeling, in keeping with the general mood of the Romantic movement. But Robert Schumann (1810–56) – although in most respects he must be reckoned among the true Romantics – embarked on a close study of the quartets of Haydn and Mozart before his great outburst of chamber-music composition in the 1840s, and for the most part his chamber works lack any kind of 'programme'. Among these works, the Quintet in E Flat major op 44 is a masterpiece specially notable for the way it unites the piano – Schumann was a fine pianist as a young man – with the conventional string quartet of two violins, viola and cello.

Johannes Brahms (1833–97) began his career as a chamber-music composer in 1853, when he wrote a movement for a sonata for violin and piano, to which his friend Schumann contributed another. Brahms' three full-scale violin sonatas are among his best-known chamber works, which also include the very successful Trio in E Flat op 40 for violin, horn and piano, a Trio for clarinet, cello and piano op 114, and a Quintet for clarinet and strings op 115, which is generally held to be his chamber-music masterpiece.

While the great works of Schumann and Brahms in this field are much less well known than they deserve to be, the slow movement of Tchaikovsky's String Quartet in D op 11 has become almost too familiar; the attractive folk song melody which occurs in it has been adapted for any number of different instruments. A similar fate has been enjoyed – if that is the word – by the tune from one of the quartets of Alexander Borodin (1833–87) which became 'And this is my beloved' in the musical *Kismet*. In fact there are many great tunes in chamber music works, Romantic or not, which deserve to be discovered by the general public. Tchaikovsky's fine pianoforte trio op 50, written 'In memory of a great artist' (Nicholas Rubinstein), is a rich store of melody, as are the many delightful chamber works of Antonín Dvořák (1841–1904), one of the best known of which is the 'American' Quartet in F op 96.

RAVEL : INTRODUCTION AND ALLEGRO FOR HARP, FLUTE, CLARINET AND STRING QUARTET

This is one of the most immediately attractive of twentieth-century chamber works, notable for the shimmering brilliance of its texture, like so much of the music of Maurice Ravel (1875–1937). It was written in 1905, two years after his string quartet, an undoubted masterwork in the form, which is often coupled in performance and compared with the only string quartet of Claude Debussy (1862–1918). Although obviously influenced here to some extent by the chamber music of César Franck (1822–90) and Gabriel Fauré (1845–1925), Debussy also drew inspiration from a far more exotic source – the iridescent sound of the Javanese gamelan orchestra.

The Ravel and Debussy quartets offer immediate musical enchantment – unlike the six quartets of Béla Bartók (1881–1945); some of these can appear spiky and aggressive at first hearing, but on further acquaintance their unusual contours become much more congenial. Spanning the period 1908–39, Bartók's six quartets display a great variety of influences, ranging from the classical style of Haydn and Mozart to the contemporary avant-garde. Although aware of the work of other composers, Bartók wrote music that was always very much his own, marked by a rhythmic vitality which is one of its chief attractions.

Today, when so many musical barriers are being broken down,

chamber music assumes an even greater variety of forms than hitherto; private patronage, which in the past gave rise to so much 'room music', has to a great extent disappeared, and the composer must look to public agencies, or to industry, for support. Chamber music, once essentially played in private, has moved into the public arena; fortunately the wider audience can be reached as more towns become endowed with the small halls suitable for its performance.

That there has long been a popular demand for chamber music was proved by the extraordinary success of the recitals given free or for a few pence by the South Place Ethical Society for so many years at the Conway Hall in London. They started in 1887, and the two-thousandth concert was held in 1969, by which time almost all the leading chamber-music performers in Britain had appeared at these recitals and many thousands of ordinary people had been given the chance to discover that chamber music was, after all, their kind of music.

4

MUSIC FOR THE SMALL ORCHESTRA

It is not growing like a tree
In bulk, doth make men better be . . .
In small proportions we just beauties see.
> Ben Jonson, 'A Pindaric Ode on the Death of
> Sir H. Morison'

HANDEL: WATER MUSIC

In the summer of 1717, King George I expressed to Baron von Kilmanseck the wish to 'have a concert on the river'. Eager to ingratiate himself, the baron made all the arrangements, which included engaging George Frideric Handel (1685–1759) to write music specially for the occasion. The king and the court embarked in one barge; in another were the musicians 'to the number of fifty, who played all kinds of instruments, viz. trumpets, hunting horns, oboes, bassoons, German flutes, French flutes à bec, violins and basses'. So much did the king approve of the music during his progress on the Thames that 'he commanded

46

it to be repeated, once before and once after supper, though it took an hour for each performance'.

Some of the numerous short pieces which make up Handel's *Water Music* became extremely popular in an arrangement for symphony orchestra by Sir Hamilton Harty; he applied similar treatment to parts of the *Music for the Royal Fireworks* which Handel composed for the celebrations in London in April 1749 to mark the Peace of Aix-la-Chapelle. He employed a massive band of forty trumpets, twenty French horns, sixteen hautboys, sixteen bassoons, eight pairs of kettledrums, twelve side-drums, and flutes and fifes; his music was about the only thing that went right, for the fireworks themselves were a disastrous flop.

Today, thanks to recordings of the music played with the appropriate number and style of instruments, the *Water Music* and the *Fireworks Music* can be heard as Handel intended them to be. The large number of musicians he used on both occasions was not typical of the period; in general the orchestras which accompanied Handel's operas and oratorios were of modest size, while the many works which he and others composed under the title 'Concerto Grosso' – literally 'big concerto' – were performed by quite a small string orchestra with harpsichord continuo and, sometimes, a group of solo instruments.

BACH : 'AIR ON THE G STRING' (SUITE IN D)

The best known of all the compositions of Johann Sebastian Bach (1685–1750) is perhaps the second movement from his third orchestral suite in D, which owes its fame to a nineteenth-century arrangement in the key of C for violin by the virtuoso August Wilhelmj (1845–1908).

The court orchestras for which Bach composed, though not large – numbering perhaps twenty musicians – were in some cases well trained. They would certainly have needed skill to cope with the complexities of his six Brandenburg Concertos, each of which was written for a different combination of instruments, as might be expected at a time when orchestras had not yet assumed a definitive shape. Nor had the word 'symphony' yet acquired its present massive connotations; it was applied to relatively brief orchestral passages in operas or oratorios, such as the 'Pastoral Symphony' in Handel's *Messiah* and the 'Sinfonia' which introduces Part Two of Bach's *Christmas Oratorio*. Symphonies written as separate entities were also short; the eight composed by William Boyce (1710–79) can all be accommodated on a single long-playing record.

Antonio Vivaldi (1678–1741) wrote an immense amount of music for the small orchestras of his time, including nearly four hundred concerti grossi. Other prolific composers of the period are known chiefly through one particular well-loved work – for instance, Johann Pachelbel (1653–1706) whose Canon in D, originally written for three violins and continuo, is familiar to many in an arrangement for string orchestra, and Tomaso Albinoni (1671–1750) whose Adagio in G minor for organ and strings owes much of its wide popularity to the twentieth-century arranger of the music, Remo Giazotto.

MOZART : EINE KLEINE NACHTMUSIK (K 525)

Eine Kleine Nachtmusik – A Little Night Music – is one of Mozart's most familiar compositions; in four short movements, for strings alone, it was completed in August 1787 and is among the large number of lighter works he wrote for entertainment purposes, often for specific occasions. The so-called 'Haffner' Serenade in D major (K 250), scored for oboes, flutes, bassoons, horns and trumpets in addition to strings, and set out in eight short movements, is rather more typical of Mozart's output in this field. It was written to celebrate the wedding in 1776 of the daughter of the burgomaster of Salzburg, Sigmund Haffner.

'Serenade' – a French word meaning 'evening music' and traditionally evoking the image of a lover singing to the object of his affections from the street below her window – was one of three terms commonly used in Mozart's time to describe works intended for performance at parties or in the open air; the others were 'divertimento' (music for diversion) and 'cassation', probably derived from the German *Gasse* (street). Instrumentation varied widely, but generally a few wind instruments would be employed together with single strings (not *groups* of violins, violas etc, as in a full orchestra). Mozart wrote a large number of chamber-orchestra works of this type, as well as innumerable dances and marches similarly scored. Haydn, too, turned out such compositions by the dozen; the eight *Notturni* (Nocturnes) produced for the King of Naples in 1790 are delightful examples of his infinite resource in writing for the chamber orchestra.

TCHAIKOVSKY : WALTZ FROM SERENADE FOR STRINGS OP 48

The composers of the nineteenth century inherited the term 'serenade' from the classical period and made their own use of it. Tchaikovsky, for instance, far from thinking of a quartet or quintet of strings, wrote a note on the score of his String Serenade, completed in 1880, saying that 'the larger the string orchestra employed, the better the composer's wishes will be met'. The graceful waltz is the best known of the work's four movements, all of them instantly appealing; no wonder Tchaikovsky's serenade was an immediate success in Russia and in London, where the composer conducted it for the Royal Philharmonic Society in 1888.

A comparable work is the enchanting Serenade in E major for Strings op 22 by Antonín Dvořák (1841–1904); this was written in 1875 when the Czech composer was thirty-four years of age and just beginning to find his mature form. Each of the five movements is attractive – Dvořák too includes a waltz – and the prevailing tone of haunting tenderness is set by the theme of the opening Moderato. The two serenades of Brahms, op 11 and op 16 – one for full orchestra and one for small orchestra – are also delightful; and among the chamber music compositions of Charles Gounod (1818–93) is the very engaging *Petite Symphonie* of 1888 for ten wind instruments.

The Norwegian composer Edvard Grieg (1843–1907) sought to recreate the musical atmosphere of earlier days when he wrote his *Holberg Suite* to mark the bicentenary of the birth in 1684 of Ludwig Holberg, the virtual founder of Danish–Norwegian literature. Originally written for piano, the suite is much better known in the composer's own arrangement for string orchestra; its six movements each have names reminiscent of Bach's time: Praeludium, Sarabande, Gavotte and Musette, Air and Rigaudon.

Among the most popular nineteenth-century works for the

49

smaller orchestra is the Serenade for Strings op 20 by Sir Edward Elgar (1857–1934), which was completed in 1892; the slow movement – Larghetto – in particular speaks eloquently of the composer's true self. As an expression of personal emotion, the 'Siegfried Idyll', composed by Richard Wagner (1813–83) for his wife Cosima, and played on the staircase outside her bedroom on Christmas Day 1870 by a small group of musicians, must surely rank among the most elegant of musical gifts.

WARLOCK : CAPRIOL SUITE

Philip Heseltine (1894–1930) used his own name for critical and editorial work in the field of old music; as Peter Warlock, he composed a good deal of vocal and instrumental music, much of it in the style of former times. The *Capriol Suite for Strings*, composed in 1926, is a lively set of dances in sixteenth-century style, based on themes from *Orchésographie*, a work by Thoinot Arbeau published in 1589. Somewhat similar in manner is the *St Paul's Suite for Strings* which Gustav Holst (1874–1934) composed in 1913 for the girls of St Paul's School, in London, where he was music master. Another work to achieve lasting fame is the Serenade for Strings op 11 by the Swedish composer Dag Wiren (b 1905). Some of the most attractive compositions of Benjamin Britten (1913–76) are scored for smaller orchestra – the early *Simple Symphony* and the *Variations on a Theme of Frank Bridge*, both composed for string orchestra, among them – while the beautiful Serenade for Tenor, Horn and Strings adds the human voice to a chamber orchestra and provides a twentieth-century interpretation of a time-honoured musical term.

5

SYMPHONIC MUSIC

As [classical] tragedy is 'serious, complete, and of a certain magnitude', a symphony deals with a high argument treated as a unity . . . its action is dramatic, and the effect of the whole on the observer should be to make him forget his own petty concerns and live for the time being on a plane of universal experience.

Grove's Dictionary of Music and Musicians, fifth edition

MOZART : FIRST MOVEMENT, SYMPHONY NO 40 IN G MINOR,
K 550 ('MOZART 40')

Ever since I was a boy playing piano-duet arrangements of Mozart's symphonies with my mother, the opening theme of his fortieth symphony has appealed strongly to me, so it was no surprise to find it rocketing to the top of the charts in a 'pop' arrangement in 1971. However, although not surprised, I was saddened by the excision of this poignant tune from its dramatic context. Mozart has been trivialised too often, and it was altogether too bad that the hacks should get their hands on his three

51

crowning symphonic achievements: the symphonies no 39 in E Flat, no 40 in G minor and no 41 in C, the 'Jupiter'.

Though he had his precursors, notably Carl Philipp Emanuel Bach (1714–88), Joseph Haydn (1732–1809) is generally thought of as the 'father' of the symphony as we know it. In his time it assumed the shape of a four-movement work; typically, the first movement would be the most weighty, the second slow-moving, the third light in character – often using the dance rhythm of the minuet – and the fourth a lively, fast finale. There were other possibilities, of course, but this was the usual pattern of the classical symphony.

Haydn wrote at least 104 symphonies, a measure of his inventive powers. Mozart was influenced by him; but, despite being the older man by nearly a quarter of a century, Haydn learned from Mozart too. The stature of the twelve magnificent symphonies Haydn wrote in the 1790s for Salomon, the London impresario, shows that he had the measure of Mozart's last three symphonic masterpieces – nos 39, 40 and 41 – which were all composed in the space of a few weeks in the summer of 1788.

Until comparatively recently Haydn's reputation with the general public as a symphonist rested on a handful of the Salomon symphonies, such as no 94 in G major, the 'Surprise', so named on account of the loud chord which suddenly interrupts the quiet flow of the slow movement; no 100 in G, the 'Military'; and no 101 in D, known as the 'Clock' from the tick-tock motion of the second movement. The Symphony no 88 in G was well known too, but most of the rest were forgotten. Fortunately the scholar H. C. Robbins Landon and the conductor Antal Dorati, among others, have stimulated a more informed interest in Haydn; all his symphonies have now been recorded, some many times, and we can discover for ourselves their infinite variety.

Mozart's encounter as a young man with the brilliant orchestra at Mannheim was a turning point in his symphonic output; it quickly bore fruit in the impressive Symphony no 31 in D major (K 297), written in Paris in 1778 and known as the 'Paris' Symphony. Of the six fine symphonies composed between 1782 and 1788, no 35 in D major (the 'Haffner'), no 36 in C major (the 'Linz') and no 38 in D major (the 'Prague') represent

Mozart at his best and were only surpassed by the three master-pieces of 1788.

The arresting four-note summons at the start of this symphony is in the rhythm of the letter 'V' in Morse code (. . . —) and was used by the BBC in its overseas broadcasts during World War II as a symbol of victory. Beethoven himself is said to have re-marked of this potent opening figure : 'That is how fate knocks at the door', and certainly Beethoven's work was a great stimulus to the idea of the 'programme' symphony – the symphony which tells a story of some kind.

Although the first two of his nine symphonies – no 1 in C major and no 2 in D major – were composed for the relatively modest orchestra of Haydn's day, they already bear Beethoven's heroic stamp. The Symphony no 3 in E Flat op 55 of 1803 was actually called *Eroica* by the composer; it is on a grand scale which was altogether new at the time. It was originally dedicated to Napoleon; but, disillusioned by evidence of Bonaparte's growing tyranny, Beethoven tore his name from the title page and substituted 'to the memory of a great man'. The first great heroic symphony, *Eroica* set a pattern which was to be followed for much of the nineteenth century and after.

Beethoven's fourth symphony, in B Flat, op 60, is slighter in form, though enchanting; the fifth is a powerful work which con-cludes in a thrilling blaze of triumph over the initial hammer-blows of fate. The Symphony no 6 in F major op 68 is the 'Pastoral'; each of its five movements has a title relating to country life, though Beethoven warned that the work was to be regarded as 'an expression of feeling rather than painting'. His seventh symphony, in A major op 92, is so full of vitality and exuberant rhythms that Wagner called it 'the apotheosis of the dance'; the eighth, op 93 in F is, in Beethoven's words, 'a little symphony', but the finale has a titanic strength which would have been quite alien to Mozart or Haydn.

There remains the great Symphony no 9 in D minor (the 'Choral') op 125; lasting well over an hour in performance, it gave a new dimension to symphonic composition, and not only because the last movement includes a setting for four soloists and chorus of Schiller's 'Ode to Joy'. The massive first movement is a symphony in itself; next comes a powerful Scherzo, followed by a long slow movement of the utmost beauty. Richard Wagner was not alone in thinking that after the 'Choral' there was no more to be done with the symphony.

SCHUBERT: SYMPHONY NO 8 IN B MINOR (THE 'UNFINISHED')

Not every work which achieves universal popularity can be called great music, but there is no doubt about Schubert's 'Unfinished' Symphony. It was begun in October 1822; two movements only were completed and, although sketches exist for a third, Schubert for some reason proceeded no further with the work before his death in 1828 at the age of thirty-one. The symphony as it stands, however, is full of haunting beauty; perhaps Schubert had, after all, said all he needed to say. Of his earlier symphonies, no 4 (the 'Tragic') is powerful though not very profound, and the popular no 5 in B Flat is full of Mozartian grace. Schubert's ninth and last symphony is, like Beethoven's, massive in scale – hence it is known as the 'Great' C major. Some consider it unduly repetitive, others would not abbreviate in any way its 'heavenly length'; but all are agreed that the finale is a movement of dazzling splendour which achieves epic stature.

None of the symphonies of Felix Mendelssohn (1809–47) which have come down to us – he wrote no fewer than seventeen – exhibits an epic quality, though the 'Italian' op 90, published in 1833, and the 'Scottish' op 56, are full of infectious energy and charm. Both were the direct result of his grand tour of Europe as a young man and developed from the musical sketchbooks of his travels.

Two of the four symphonies of Robert Schumann (1810–56) also drew inspiration from the world around him: no 1 in B Flat, originally called 'A Spring Symphony', and no 3 in E Flat, the 'Rhenish', which has a slow movement suggested by a ceremony in Cologne Cathedral. It was Hector Berlioz (1803–69) who first used the symphonic form to tell a definite, biographical story. The *Symphonie Fantastique* of 1830 is subtitled 'Episodes from the life of an artist' and culminates in the thrilling nightmare of the witches' sabbath; *Harold in Italy* (1834), with its important part for solo viola, is based on episodes from Byron's poem 'Childe Harold', while *Romeo and Juliet* (1839), based on Shakespeare's play, enlarges the concept of the symphony almost beyond recognition. It includes vocal solos as well as choral episodes, while the music of the love scene, Capulet's ball and the 'Queen Mab' Scherzo – directly inspired by Mercutio's speech – have well-deserved places in the orchestral repertoire.

MAHLER: ADAGIETTO, SYMPHONY NO 5

Gustav Mahler (1860–1911) completed nine large-scale symphonies and left a tenth unfinished. Following the example of Beethoven and Berlioz, he used voices in these works whenever it suited his purpose and expressed through symphonic music the story of his own tragic experience of life. Twenty-five years ago it was possible to state that in most countries 'a small but important band of [Mahler] enthusiasts contends with a multitude of detractors'; now his works are usually performed to packed audiences, some of whom were perhaps introduced to Mahler's infinitely seductive music by hearing part of the moving slow movement of his fifth symphony in Luchino Visconti's film *Death in Venice*.

A strong feeling for nature and for song runs through the first four of Mahler's symphonies; nos 5–7, purely orchestral, are concerned with the struggles of the human soul; no 8 is the 'Symphony of a Thousand', so called from the number of performers required for this devotional epic; no 9 and no 10 are again orchestral works. There is also the deeply moving *Song of the Earth*, based on Chinese poems, for tenor and contralto soloists with orchestra; this is described by Mahler as a symphony, which is consistent with the composer's own definition of the word: 'for me, symphony means the building of a world by means of every available technical resource'.

Those words might apply equally well to Wagner's concept of opera; indeed, for Wagner, opera had taken over the role of the symphony as the most total form of musical expression since the supreme achievement of Beethoven's Ninth. For Anton

Bruckner (1824–96), influenced though he was by Wagner's opulent methods, this was not so. Bruckner coupled a Schubertian gift for melody with a profoundly religious view of life; both found an outlet in his expansive symphonies. Those published in his lifetime are numbered, like Beethoven's, from one to nine.

Destined to be Beethoven's symphonic successor was Johannes Brahms (1833–97); the knowledge that he was expected to produce a work worthy to follow Beethoven's Ninth weighed him down for years. It was not until he was forty-three that Brahms managed to complete his first symphony, in C minor op 68; it is a magnificent abstract work, as are his other three symphonies – no 2 in D op 73, no 3 in F op 90 and no 4 in E minor op 98. Without adopting a programme of any kind, these splendid compositions exploit to the full the capacity of symphonic form to express heroic themes and heroic struggles, to assert the triumph of the human spirit.

TCHAIKOVSKY : SLOW MOVEMENT, SYMPHONY NO 5 IN E MINOR OP 64

The genesis of the Romantic approach to the symphony can be found in the days of Haydn and Mozart, when symphonic first movements – and sometimes other symphonic movements – came to be cast in what is known as 'sonata form'; as the name suggests, this form was shared with instrumental sonatas of the period. Reduced to its simplest elements, 'sonata form' movements consist of the statement of tune 'A' followed by the statement of a contrasting tune 'B'; then follows a section in which these thematic ideas are developed in contrast with each other, and a final section in which the themes are restated. This simple pattern could, in imaginative hands, provide the basis of dramatic conflict in musical terms; and, more often than not, the first movement constitutes the symphony's most dramatic component.

By the time of Peter Tchaikovsky (1840–93) many variations had been introduced into the symphonic pattern. His last three symphonies (no 4 in F minor op 36, no 5, and no 6 in B minor) are in a sense episodes in a musical autobiography, reflecting the composer's own struggles against a hostile destiny – indeed, both the fourth and fifth symphonies are dominated by a theme representing fate. The beguiling horn melody which opens the slow movement of the fifth symphony is one of several passages in Tchaikovsky to be purloined by the world of pop music – no wonder, for his works are full of instant melodic appeal as well as dramatic power. Incidentally, those who enjoy Tchaikovsky's music will almost certainly respond to the emotional richness of the symphony in D minor by the French composer César Franck (1822–90); like so many Romantic symphonies it is a tale of dark struggle brought to a triumphant conclusion.

Tchaikovsky was by no means the only Russian symphonic composer of importance. Probably the first Russian symphony was composed by Nicholas Rimsky-Korsakov (1844–1908), who wrote three in all but is more often remembered by the symphonic suite *Scheherazade*, based on the *Arabian Nights*. Symphony no 2 in B minor by Alexander Borodin (1837–87) rivals Tchaikovsky's symphonies in popularity, and his work is even more securely rooted in the soil of Russian folk music.

DVOŘÁK : LARGO, SYMPHONY NO 9 IN E MINOR OP 95
('FROM THE NEW WORLD')

The slow movement of Dvořák's E minor symphony is one of the most famous pieces in the entire symphonic repertoire; the work as a whole contains references to the folk music of the United States, where the symphony was written, but even more apparent are borrowings from Bohemian melody and rhythm: Antonín Dvořák (1841–1904) was clearly addressing a musical message from the New World to his European homeland. Of Dvořák's other symphonies, only no 8 in G major op 88 approaches the popularity of the 'New World'.

In common with many other composers of the Romantic period, Dvořák's symphonic output was not confined to symphonies. The concert overture had by this time become in effect a one-movement symphony; Dvořák wrote three : 'In Nature's Realm', 'Carnival' and 'Othello', which form a cycle called *Nature, Life and Love*. And there was also the symphonic poem, of which Dvořák wrote five based on folk ballads.

Dvořák's fellow-countryman Bedřich Smetana (1824–84) wrote a magnificent series of six symphonic poems in celebration of their native Bohemia under the general title *My Country*; the best known is 'From Bohemia's Woods and Fields'. Smetana was directly inspired by the example of Franz Liszt (1811–86) who invented the concept of the symphonic poem with the deliberate intention of bringing literary, dramatic and pictorial ideas into music. The titles of Liszt's two symphonies – *Dante* and *Faust* – show their literary origin clearly enough, and his one-movement symphonic poems were based on, among others, Byron, Goethe, Lamartine and Shakespeare.

DUKAS : THE SORCERER'S APPRENTICE

Paul Dukas (1865–1935) described his most famous work as a scherzo – a musical joke – but it is essentially a symphonic poem; it is based on the story by Goethe about the lazy apprentice who bewitches a broomstick into fetching water for him and is nearly drowned when he forgets the magic formula to make it stop. The music achieved even greater popularity when Walt Disney cast Mickey Mouse as the apprentice in the film *Fantasia*. First performed in 1897, *The Sorcerer's Apprentice* is a good example of 'programme music' at its most vivid; the bassoon brilliantly plays the role of the broomstick, and is joined by another, to comic effect, when the apprentice breaks the broomstick in half.

In the course of a century, since the days of Haydn, the symphony orchestra had become an enormous affair, often with a hundred players or more. No orchestral composer more fully relished the opportunities afforded by this vast canvas than Richard Strauss (1864–1949). In his work for the operatic stage and concert platform the flower of the Romantic movement became decidedly full-blown, but the colour is all the more gorgeous. Strauss' most familiar orchestral work, *Till Eulenspiegel's Merry Pranks*, was written at almost exactly the same time as *The Sorcerer's Apprentice* and shares its sense of humour. The superb *Don Juan* op 20 reflects the youthful fire of its twenty-four-year-old composer; *Death and Transfiguration*, *A Hero's Life* and *Thus spake Zarathustra* are symphonic poems on a more massive scale, while the composer's humour again shows through in *Don Quixote* and the *Sinfonia Domestica* –

58

whose 'programme' is quite simply the daily routine of Strauss family life.

ELGAR: 'NIMROD' FROM THE 'ENIGMA' VARIATIONS OP 36

Richard Strauss was one of the first great continental musical figures to recognise the stature of Edward Elgar (1857–1934) when his oratorio *The Dream of Gerontius* was performed at Düsseldorf in 1901. This followed closely on the enormous success of the *Variations on an Original Theme for Orchestra* – known as the 'Enigma' Variations – first given in 1899; the enigma of Elgar's theme still remains, for he teasingly declared that, quite apart from the one stated at the outset, another theme 'goes' through the work. What comes across with unequivocal clarity is the marvellous portrait gallery of the composer's 'friends pictured within'; each variation depicts a different character in the Elgar circle. 'Nimrod', the best-known variation, is dedicated to A. J. Jaeger, the composer's publisher (Jäger is the German word for huntsman, and Nimrod was the biblical hunter).

For many years, trifles like *Chanson de Matin* and the almost disastrously popular *Pomp and Circumstance* marches, including the tune for 'Land of Hope and Glory', obscured Elgar's great symphonic gifts. Now, fortunately – not least through the advocacy of Sir Adrian Boult on the conductor's rostrum – his two symphonies, no 1 in A Flat op 55 and no 2 in E Flat op 63, are recognised for the magnificent works they are.

Sergei Rachmaninoff (1873–1943) suffered a similar disadvantage in his lifetime: one or two of his pieces, in particular the early Prelude in C Sharp minor, occupied a disproportionate amount of public attention. Today the merits of his three symphonies, op 13, 27 and 44, are widely appreciated, together with other major though less well known compositions such as *The Bells*, a choral work based on Edgar Allan Poe's poem.

SIBELIUS: FINLANDIA

Jean Sibelius (1865–1957) is a symphonic composer whose stature is still debated. On one level he was the supreme patriot who, in *Finlandia* (1899), caught his country's mood of defiance;

this is only one, and not the most musically impressive, of his symphonic poems founded on national life and legend. Others are the haunting *Swan of Tuonela* (one of four *Legends from the Kalevala*), *The Oceanides* and *Tapiola*. But Sibelius also wrote seven symphonies, of which no 2 in D and no 5 in E Flat have achieved special fame; no 7 in C, a single-movement work of great power, is often performed.

The reputation of Sibelius's Danish contemporary Carl Nielsen (1865–1931) has grown steadily on the international scene. Of his six symphonies, no 4, the 'Inextinguishable', has achieved a regular place in the repertoire, with its highly individual blend of romanticism and Nordic toughness.

Ralph Vaughan Williams (1872–1958), one of the major symphonic composers of the twentieth century, drew much inspiration from English folk-song and music of medieval and Renaissance times. *A Lark Ascending*, a beautiful symphonic poem with an important solo violin part, is among the best known of his many orchestral compositions, which include nine symphonies. Some of his works are programmatic, like the early *Sea Symphony* (no 1), *London Symphony* (no 2), *Pastoral Symphony* (no 3) and the *Sinfonia Antarctica* (no 7), based on the score he wrote for the film *Scott of the Antarctic*; others are abstract, intensely personal in expression.

PROKOFIEV : CLASSICAL SYMPHONY

The extension of symphonic form to the ultimate in scale and expressive power during the Romantic era was bound, sooner or later, to lead to a reaction, and in the early years of the twentieth century it came, not least in the work of Igor Stravinsky (1882–1971). One important ingredient in his complex musical personality was an interest in pre-Romantic forms of music – an interest shared by Serge Prokofiev (1891–1953), whose *Classical Symphony* of 1916–17 was perhaps the most popular product of the neo-classical trend. In fact, like that of Stravinsky, Prokofiev's style shows many influences, among them pressure from the Soviet state to write music in conformity with Communist ideals; it is a measure of his courage and mastery that he produced so much of lasting value. Dimitri Shostakovich (1906–

1975) likewise had to endure periods of ostracism when his work was criticised for 'ideological deficiencies'; in the world outside Russia his reputation as a major composer in many fields has grown apace, with no 5 and no 7 (the 'Leningrad'), of his fifteen symphonies, becoming particularly popular.

Among modern British composers, William Walton (b 1902) and Benjamin Britten (1913–76) stand out in several areas of music. Walton's two symphonies display the fastidious mixture of brilliance and lyricism that makes concert overtures like *Scapino* and *Portsmouth Point* so enjoyable. Britten, prolific in operatic composition, has written relatively little in symphonic form; the *Sinfonia da Requiem* and the Cello Symphony are among his few symphonic works.

Is the symphony dead or dying? Many composers, from Wagner onwards, have said so. The fact is that, however much the form has changed, the name 'Symphony' still presents the supreme challenge to a composer; Peter Maxwell Davies is said to have hesitated painfully before deciding to apply the title to a major new orchestral work first performed in 1977.

6

THE CONCERTO

The conquered pianos lie scattered around him, broken strings float like trophies, wounded instruments flee in all directions. And he . . . smiles strangely before this crowd that applauds him madly.

A contemporary view of Liszt, quoted in
Sydney Harrison, *Grand Piano*, 1976

VIVALDI: THE FOUR SEASONS

The term 'concerto' conveys to most people a large-scale work for a virtuoso soloist and full orchestra, but it did not always have that meaning. Both 'concert' and the Italian equivalent 'concerto' were used to describe a musical occasion in which more than one performer shared the music-making, and also when referring to the group of players itself. In the late seventeenth century, Arcangelo Corelli (1653–1713) and other Italian violinist-composers developed a form of concerto in which a small group of strings – the 'concertante' strings – alternated with a larger section – the 'ripieno' strings. The 'concerto grosso', devised by Corelli on this pattern, was used to great effect by Handel and Bach. The six Brandenburg Concertos belong to this type of composition; dedicated by Bach to the Margrave of Brandenburg in 1721, each of the concertos employs different instruments, including a flute, recorders, oboes, trumpets, horns and bassoons, as well as strings.

Bach learned a good deal about string composition from his near contemporary Antonio Vivaldi (1678–1741), who wrote nearly four hundred works bearing the title 'Concerto' in a great variety of styles and for varying groups of instruments. Many of these concertos foreshadow the modern shape of such compositions by using a single solo instrument plus accompanying orchestra; among them are the famous quartet of violin concertos named after the four seasons of the year. These highly descriptive works, each prefaced by a poem appropriate to the season in question, remind us that programme music was by no means an invention of the Romantic era, and that composers had long been tempted to imitate the sounds of nature.

MOZART : SLOW MOVEMENT, PIANO CONCERTO NO 21 IN C
(K 467)

By the end of the eighteenth century, the concerto had evolved decisively into a work in three movements, of which the first was the most weighty, the second slow and lyrical, and the third quick – a work for one soloist (occasionally two, exceptionally three) with orchestra. The greatest master of concerto writing at this time was undoubtedly Wolfgang Amadeus Mozart (1756–91). Among his many works in this form, he wrote five violin concertos, four for the horn and twenty-five for piano and orchestra. The piano concertos occupy a very special place in Mozart's output, ranging in mood from the dark intensity of the Concerto in C minor (K 491) to the untroubled serenity of the well-known Concerto in A major (K 488). The haunting slow movement of the Concerto no 21 in C (K 467) became familiar to a wider public through its use as background music in the film *Elvira Madigan*. Those who know Mozart's concertos only through this single piece are strongly urged to explore further; they will come across an infinite variety of deeply expressive music and will sooner or later discover the enchanting Concerto for Flute and Harp (K 299) which is one of the most immediately appealing of all concertos.

BEETHOVEN: PIANO CONCERTO NO 5 IN E FLAT OP 73 ('EMPEROR')

Mozart, as his symphonies demonstrate, was a master of the orchestra; the long line of his concertos develops with progressive subtlety the quality of dialogue between soloist and orchestra which belongs in a special way to concerto form. Musical questions are asked and answers supplied; sometimes the conversation is calm, sometimes heated. Frequently soloist and orchestra echo each other in amiable fashion, but contradictions often occur. The form in fact revealed, in Mozart's hands, its *dramatic* possibilities. The drama of the concerto, however, is of a different kind from that of its close relative the symphony; here, instead of the interaction of a group of protagonists, we have the single figure against many, the orator swaying the crowd. The concerto form contained elements which were to appeal strongly to the romantic imagination.

Beethoven's first two piano concertos, in C major and B Flat, are fortified Mozart; the last three – in C minor, G major and E Flat major (the 'Emperor') – belong to Beethoven's own new world, passionate and powerful. The brief central slow movement of the Piano Concerto no 4 in G major was likened by Liszt to Orpheus taming the wild beasts with his music; in it the quiet but assured tones of the piano gradually gain control over the rugged voice of the orchestra.

In Beethoven's last great piano concerto, in E Flat, whose noble quality gave rise to its nickname, the 'Emperor', victory belongs to neither side. Piano and orchestra appear as equal partners in one of the finest of all concertos. Beethoven's glorious Violin Concerto in D major is to the violin what the 'Emperor' is to the piano, making full use of the more lyrical character of the instrument and solving to perfection the quite different problems of balance involved. There is also Beethoven's Triple Concerto for violin, cello, piano and orchestra – an impressive curiosity.

The towering stature of Beethoven inevitably overshadows his contemporaries in the field of the concerto as in other areas of music, but the achievement of Carl Maria Weber (1786–1826) in his works for piano and orchestra and for clarinet and orchestra must not be forgotten; and the merits of the piano concertos of Johann Nepomuk Hummel (1778–1837) have been rediscovered of late.

MENDELSSOHN : VIOLIN CONCERTO IN E MINOR

With Beethoven, the concerto began to assume the Romantic form in which it is most familiar to us – conveying the image of an adored virtuoso, by turns tender and tremendous, overwhelming the public with his expressive and technical prowess. However, in the single piano concerto of Robert Schumann (1810–56) and the two of Frédéric Chopin (1810–49), technical brilliance is at the service of true feeling; Schumann's concerto in A minor is an enchanting masterpiece and in Chopin's concertos the slow movements, in particular, are of such lyrical beauty that the composer's somewhat limited ability in writing for the orchestra is soon overlooked. In the two piano concertos of Felix Mendelssohn (1809–47), the element of display is rather more marked, but his single violin concerto, in E minor op 64, is a wonderfully satisfying composition from every point of view. It is rare among concertos in having four movements, though the third is very short – only fourteen bars; the chief glory of the work is the exquisitely lyrical slow movement which is probably the main reason for its universal popularity.

LISZT : HUNGARIAN FANTASIA

Franz Liszt (1811–86) was a visionary innovator in many areas of music, not least in compositions for the piano, with or without orchestra. Probably the best known of his concerto-type pieces is the *Hungarian Fantasia*, based on the fourteenth of the *Hungarian Rhapsodies*, but he also wrote two piano concertos –

no 1 in E Flat and no 2 in A major. Each is in a single continuous movement with contrasting sections, and, as might be expected from a performer of such incomparable brilliance, they present many technical difficulties. One of the most potent influences on Liszt as a young man was Niccolò Paganini; Liszt made up his mind to do for the piano what Paganini had done for the violin, and there is a comparable display of virtuosity in many of Liszt's piano works. However, there is a good deal more depth in Liszt's two piano concertos – particularly the poetic no 2 – than there is in the violin concertos of Paganini, brilliant though these are.

BRUCH : VIOLIN CONCERTO IN G MINOR OP 26

Max Bruch, who was born in Cologne in 1838 and died near Berlin in 1920, was a successful conductor as well as a composer (he directed the concerts of the Liverpool Philharmonic Society for a time); but he is now best remembered for a moving work for cello and orchestra, *Kol Nidrei*, and for the first of his two violin concertos, a work of great melodic appeal which has won a special place in the affections of music lovers.

For all its lyrical charm and popularity, his G minor violin concerto hardly aspires to the stature of the concertos of Bruch's near-contemporary, Johannes Brahms (1833–97). The Violin Concerto in D major op 77, which Brahms wrote for the virtuoso Joseph Joachim (1831–1907), is a great masterpiece; his two piano concertos, no 1 in D minor op 15 and no 2 in B Flat op 83, are massive works of symphonic weight (though in his perversely humorous way Brahms described the second as a 'tiny tiny wisp of a concerto'); and finally there is the beautiful 'double' concerto in A minor op 102 for violin, cello and orchestra, ranging in mood from exuberance to the utmost lyrical tenderness.

GRIEG : PIANO CONCERTO IN A MINOR OP 16

Liszt was such a dominant figure in the musical Europe of his time that a word of encouragement from him could make all the difference to a young composer's morale and reputation. Such was the case with Edvard Grieg (1843–1907); when he met Liszt in Rome in 1870, the great man played through Grieg's A minor piano concerto (composed two years earlier) at sight, reacting with enthusiasm to the work and commenting: 'Keep on, I tell you. You have what is needed, and don't let them frighten you.'

Grieg's single piano concerto, one of the most famous in the entire repertoire, is tuneful and exciting, with refreshing echoes of Norwegian folk music. In central Europe, Antonín Dvořák (1841–1904) too absorbed the folk idioms of his native land; they found expression in many of his works, not least the glorious Cello Concerto in B minor op 104.

TCHAIKOVSKY: PIANO CONCERTO NO 1 IN B FLAT MINOR OP 23

There have been many instances of a work failing at its first hearing yet subsequently achieving great popularity, but seldom can a composer have suffered such a shattering blow as did Peter Tchaikovsky (1840–93) when Nicholas Rubinstein, his friend and revered master, pronounced his first piano concerto to be worthless and unplayable, with only a very few passages of any merit. Fortunately the composer's depression was lifted by the resounding success of its first public performance by Hans von Bülow at Boston, Mass., in 1875. How many young people, I wonder, have been drawn to a love of music by the thrilling introductory D Flat chords and the sweeping melody which opens this concerto?

Tchaikovsky's second piano concerto, in G major, is also an exhilarating piece, though it cannot compare with the first for variety of inspiration. One of the most enjoyable of all violin concertos, however, is Tchaikovsky's masterly work in D op 35.

Tchaikovsky found a kindred spirit in the French composer Camille Saint-Saëns (1835–1921); the second and fourth of his five piano concertos are the most popular. The Belgian César Franck (1822–1890) wrote no piano concertos as such, but his *Symphonic Variations* for piano and orchestra is a delightful and well loved work in concerto idiom. Of all concerto-esque pieces perhaps the best known is the Scherzo from the *Concerto Symphonique* by Henri Litolff (1818–1891).

67

The enormous popular success some few of Rachmaninoff's works had in his lifetime is not likely to last, and musicians never regarded it with much favour . . . his music is well constructed and effective, but monotonous in texture, which consists in essence mainly of artificial and gushing tunes accompanied by a variety of figures derived from arpeggios.

Grove's Dictionary of Music and Musicians, fifth edition

There was indeed a period when, perhaps partly as a result of his 'enormous popular success', Sergei Rachmaninoff (1873–1943) fell into disfavour with intellectuals, but that time is past. The merit of his output is now widely recognised, ranging as it does from some most beautiful songs to big choral and orchestral compositions.

Although his second piano concerto may have suffered from over-exposure, in the hands of a fine pianist it has lost none of its appeal. The sombre opening, like the melancholy tolling of bells, leads to a flood of romantic melody such as few other composers could produce. The Piano Concerto no 3 in D minor op 30 was written in 1901 for Rachmaninoff's first visit to the USA, which was to become his home after the Russian Revolution. More highly esteemed by performers than his second piano concerto, it is hardly less popular with the public; it has a slow movement of great lyrical beauty and the big tune of the finale never fails to lift the heart. The first of Rachmaninoff's piano concertos is a most attractive work which is less widely known than it deserves to be, but the fourth and last has never been entirely successful.

One other work for piano and orchestra by Rachmaninoff has achieved great popularity: the *Rhapsody on a Theme of Paganini,* written in 1934. This is really a set of variations on one of Paganini's caprices for violin, the sensuous Variation no 18 being especially well loved.

ELGAR : VIOLIN CONCERTO IN B MINOR OP 61

Sir Edward Elgar (1857–1934) wrote two great concertos: one for cello in 1919, and one for violin, dedicated to Fritz Kreisler and first performed by him in 1910. The violin concerto is probably known to the musical public of today mainly through its association with Yehudi Menuhin. In November 1932 Sir Edward, then aged seventy-five, conducted a historic recording of the concerto with the fifteen-year-old prodigy as soloist; in spite of the limited technical resources then at the disposal of recording engineers, the record, which is still available, remains one of the finest of all interpretations of the work. Yehudi Menuhin, in his book *Unfinished Journey* (Macdonald & Jane's, 1976), recalls how he first met Elgar in the summer of 1932. At Grosvenor House in London early one Saturday afternoon, with his accompanist Ivor Newton, the young Menuhin nervously awaited the arrival of the great composer for a first run-through of the solo part:

> At two o'clock, Ivor and I were in place when Sir Edward arrived, a composer such as I was not prepared for: composers in my experience were Biblical prophets (Bloch) or heroes of chivalry (Enesco), not grandfatherly country gentlemen who should properly have had a couple of hounds gambolling at their heels and whose attitude to duty seemed, to say the least, relaxed. Ivor and I started to play at the soloist's entry and hadn't even reached the 'English' second theme when Sir Edward stopped us: he was sure the recording would go beautifully and meanwhile, if we would excuse him, he was off to the races!

Elgar's concerto is a work of profound beauty. On the title page an inscription reads: 'Aquì està encerrada el alma de . . .' – 'Here lies buried the soul of . . .' – whom? Elgar, always fond of riddles, still keeps us guessing.

Composers have made as much use of the concerto as a musical form in the twentieth century as in previous times. Béla Bartók (1881–1945) was long thought to be a composer of forbidding modernity; now, however, the brilliance of his piano concertos is widely appreciated, and his Concerto for Orchestra – featuring soloists from different sections – is well established in the concert repertoire. The first of Serge Prokofiev's five piano concertos, in D Flat, is particularly popular, with its almost Tchaikovskian quality; Sir William Walton (born 1902) has written fine concertos for violin and viola, and Malcolm Arnold (born 1921) has composed a number of such works for a variety of instruments.

7

SONGS

Forget not, brother singer, that though Prose
Can never be too truthful or too wise,
Song is not Truth, nor Wisdom, but the rose
Upon Truth's lips, the light in Wisdom's eyes.

Sir William Watson (1858–1935), 'Ode to J. C. Collins'

TRADITIONAL : 'THE FOGGY DEW'

Song of one kind or another is almost as ancient as the human
voice itself, but the earliest songs can never be known to us;
they vanished long before musical notation was thought of or,
in the course of centuries, became unrecognisable in the process
of being passed from 'mouth to mouth'. The origins of folk songs
are often obscure; seldom can they be traced to any specific
composer, and they frequently appear in many variations of tune
and words, differing from place to place and from time to time.
This is not surprising, as the human memory was the only means
of acquiring and preserving songs and the old singers, being

creators in their own right, would feel no qualms about making changes to suit themselves or their listeners.

It was in the eighteenth century, with the rapid growth of large towns, that educated people in the British Isles began to take an interest in the music of the countryside, perhaps because it seemed already under threat. George Thomson of Edinburgh (1757–1851), a remarkable collector of the period, was able to persuade Haydn, Beethoven and Weber, among others, to write accompaniments for the tunes he gathered from Scotland, Ireland and Wales. In the latter part of the nineteenth century and the early years of the twentieth, there were folk-song collectors who would have deplored Thomson's approach; their concern was to set down without adornment the words and tunes they heard from the lips of country folk. A leading figure in this carefully authentic approach to folk music was Cecil Sharp (1859–1924), who collected many hundreds of songs in the British Isles and the USA.

The use of folk songs by educated composers goes back to the beginnings of music as we know it – indeed it is often difficult to disentangle what is composed from what is merely absorbed. To take just one example, 'The Foggy Dew' is probably best known today through the arrangement with piano accompaniment by Benjamin Britten; but, according to A. L. Lloyd in his *Folk Song in England*, Britten used a tune of Dutch origin instead of the one commonly sung in East Anglia which is closely related to the melody of 'Ye Banks and Braes'. As for the words, there are many known variants; a version noted in the early nineteenth century speaks of the apprentice lad hauling his girl friend into bed to shield her from 'the Bogle bo' – a ghost of his own unscrupulous invention. Those who would explore the complex world of folk song, beware!

PURCELL : 'FAIREST ISLE'

During the reign of Queen Elizabeth I, there were times and places where the amusements of rich and poor almost coincided – as in Shakespeare's Globe Theatre; but in the latter part of the seventeenth century, after the Restoration of the monarchy, theatrical entertainments had become far more exclusive affairs.

In the summer of 1691, at London's Dorset Gardens Theatre, *King Arthur or The British Worthy* was staged; a typical product of the period, it was written by John Dryden with incidental music by Henry Purcell. Elaborate transformation scenes and figures from classical antiquity feature in this account of a legendary British hero; the play's most famous song is allotted to the goddess of love:

> Fairest Isle, all isles excelling,
> Seat of pleasures, and of loves;
> Venus here will choose her dwelling,
> And forsake her Cyprian groves . . .

It is a measure of Purcell's genius that he was able to transcend the cardboard theatrical conventions of the period by composing music of originality for such plays. The concluding masque in *King Arthur*, the masque in *Diocletian* (1690) and much of the music for *The Fairy Queen* (1692, adapted from Shakespeare's *A Midsummer Night's Dream*) – including the amusing scene of the drunken poet – would establish Purcell's greatness as a composer for the theatre, even if he had never written his single true opera, *Dido and Aeneas*. One short piece of his incidental music – the Rondeau from *Abdelazar, or the Moor's Revenge* – has achieved special fame through its use by Benjamin Britten in his *Variations on a Theme of Purcell*, otherwise known as *The Young Person's Guide to the Orchestra*.

Patriotic sentiments akin to those of 'Fairest Isle' were commonplace in the plays and masques of Purcell's time and continued to inspire the poets and composers of the succeeding generation. Thomas Arne (1710–78), remembered for his settings of Shakespearean songs like 'Where the Bee sucks' and 'Under the Greenwood Tree', is known above all for 'Rule, Britannia'; this first appeared in the masque *Alfred*, performed at a garden party given by the Prince of Wales in August 1740.

BALFE: 'EXCELSIOR!'

In Victorian times popular music-making centred on the home; gathered around the parlour piano, all who could sing (and many who could not) were encouraged to render their repertoire of ballads. These were not ballads in the original 'folk' sense of the word, but the story-songs turned out in hundreds and thousands to cater for the home-music market of this period. Patriotism was still a major theme : songs and 'piano fantasias' celebrated the triumphs of British troops in far-off Africa and India, though few were as effective as John Braham's 'The Death of Nelson' in commemorating the nation's heroes. Death, in tales of love or war, played its tragic role in many Victorian ballads, reflecting the cruel uncertainties of life before the advent of modern medical knowledge. Children commonly died in infancy, and mothers in childbirth, and the ballad-makers dwelt with almost gruesome tenderness on such griefs; but invariably there was another world beyond the sky to which the loved ones had departed, where they were happy in a way that had never been possible 'here below', and where, in due course, they would be reunited with those who mourned their loss. A good example of Victorian pathos is Ezra Read's 'Which is the Way to Heaven?', in which two street urchins – a boy and a girl – ask a 'bobby' to tell them how to walk to heaven, for they cannot afford the train fare : 'Mother has gone to live there, sir', they explain, 'And Daddy's so ill today'. In verse two, the boy has already been killed in a street accident, and the little girl, with her dying breath, once again enquires the way to heaven. We know she will be there all too soon.

By no means all Victorian songs are so depressing; many are vigorous and stirring, like the duet 'Excelsior!', a setting by Michael Balfe (1808–70) of words by Longfellow. The song reflects Balfe's feeling for drama; the Irish-born composer wrote one of the most popular of all operas in English, *The Bohemian Girl*, and was also successful as a London theatre manager.

IRELAND : 'SEA FEVER'

John Ireland (1879–1962) wrote many songs and piano pieces which are distinctively 'English' in feeling. 'Sea Fever', a setting of John Masefield's poem which begins 'I must go down to the seas again', achieved a quite exceptional success; in 1925, radio listeners voted it the most popular of all broadcast songs, and it is still in the repertoire of many concert singers.

Ireland – whose work is now being heard again to a much greater extent than in recent years – was a near contemporary of Ralph Vaughan Williams (1872–1958), who devoted much time as a young man to the study and collection of English folk songs. The famous 'Linden Lea' is only one of his many compositions for solo voice; again the atmosphere of the music as well as the words suggests the open air and the English countryside. These qualities are common to other twentieth-century songs by such composers as Ivor Gurney (1890–1937), George Butterworth (1885–1916), Herbert Howells (b 1892) and Benjamin Britten (1913–76).

SCHUBERT : 'DIE FORELLE' (THE TROUT)

Before the turn of the century it was to the continent of Europe that everyone looked for musical inspiration. It was not just because Queen Victoria had married a German prince that the language and musical tradition of Germany commanded the highest respect. Sir Arthur Sullivan (1842–1900) went to the Royal Academy of Music with the help of a scholarship established by Mendelssohn, and chose to continue his studies at Leipzig University; subsequently, on a journey to Vienna in 1862, he helped rediscover some of Schubert's lost manuscripts. Good though many of Sullivan's songs are, they never quite achieve a Schubertian quality.

Franz Schubert (1797–1828) composed over six hundred songs; on a single day in October 1815 he wrote eight and, in the course of that year, 144. Using the work mainly of contemporary Romantic poets, Schubert was able to illuminate his texts with a vocal line of uncanny aptitude, writing piano accompaniments which frequently contribute as much as the voice to the effectiveness of the songs. 'The Erl King' owes its appeal to a great extent to the highly dramatic accompaniment, and the piano part of 'The Trout' delightfully suggests the playful leaping movements of the fish in the water. Some of Schubert's finest creations are to be found in song-cycles – sequences of songs which tell a story – like *Die schöne Müllerin* (The Beautiful Mill-girl) and *Die Winterreise* (The Winter Journey).

Robert Schumann (1810–56) wrote several song-cycles – perhaps the best known is *Frauenliebe und -leben* (Woman's Life and Love) – and numerous songs besides. Lieder – the word simply means 'songs', but has come to be associated particularly with German art songs of the nineteenth century – were also composed by Johannes Brahms (1833–97), Hugo Wolf (1860–1903 and Richard Strauss (1864–1949).

HAHN: 'SI MES VERS AVAIENT DES AILES'

The art of song has flourished in France at least as vigorously as in Germany, dating back to the infinitely varied 'chansons' of the Middle Ages. Reynaldo Hahn belongs to the French tradition by adoption: born in Venezuela in 1875, he lived most of his life in France and died in Paris in 1947. 'Si mes vers avaient des ailes' (If my Verses had Wings) is one of the best known of the very large number of French art songs produced in the late nineteenth and early twentieth centuries; refined in sentiment, they can sound rather arch if not well performed, but a great artist such as Dame Maggie Teyte – who was one of the major interpreters of the French vocal repertoire – can make them infinitely expressive.

Georges Bizet (1838–75) wrote some fifty songs, 'Chanson d'Avril' (April Song) and 'Adieux de l'Hôtesse Arabe' (The Arab Hostess's Farewell) being among the most attractive. The set of songs called *Nuits d'Eté* (Summer Nights) by Hector Berlioz (1803–69) are exquisite; Gabriel Fauré (1845–1924) wrote many notable songs, and the fame of Henri Duparc (1848–1933) rests on a dozen songs and virtually nothing more. Among the many other creators of French art songs, Maurice Ravel (1875–1937) and Claude Debussy (1862–1918) cannot be omitted.

COTTRAU: 'SANTA LUCIA'

When Paolo Tosti (1846–1916) became singing master to Britain's royal family – he was knighted for his work in 1908 – a strong link was forged with Italian popular music; 'Goodbye!', a setting of words by the former guardsman G. J. Whyte-Melville, was only one of Tosti's many successful ballads. The great Italian tenor Enrico Caruso (1873–1921), who began recording in 1902 and made an estimated £600,000 from his gramophone records, helped to familiarise the world with the vast repertoire of Italian popular songs.

Caruso was born in the poor quarter of Naples and grew up among the Neapolitan songs he was later to sing with such passion and artistry; a collection of these is still happily available on record – Ember GVC 6. 'Santa Lucia', probably the best-known of all Neapolitan songs, was sung to great effect by Caruso's successor as the world's leading Italian operatic tenor, Beniamino Gigli (1890–1957), and has featured in the repertoire of many other vocalists, good and bad. The words and music were written by Teodor Cottrau, who was born in Naples in 1827 and died there in 1879; apart from being a composer and lyricist, he was also a publisher, and 'Santa Lucia' first appeared in a collection of Neapolitan songs produced by his firm in 1850.

Spain is another rich source of popular songs, and Spanish singers like Victoria de los Angeles and Teresa Berganza have done much through their concerts to make this repertoire known to the musical public all over the world.

THE VOLGA BOAT SONG

What Caruso did for the popular music of Italy, the great bass Feodor Chaliapin (1873–1938) achieved for the Russian repertoire, both inside and outside the opera house. In *The Gramophone Jubilee Book* (General Gramophone Publications, 1973) F. W. Gaisberg – who first recorded Chaliapin in 1902 – recalled how his most famous song was created :

Chaliapin had played as a boy on the banks of the Volga and swum in its waters . . . he frequently saw the toilers on the banks of the river, hauling great barges upstream to the accompaniment of a monotonous chant . . . I knew that this early experience was the foundation of his intense sympathy with the life and aspirations of the Russian worker, and therefore suggested he should give the outside world an impression of that early environment by singing 'The Song of the Volga Boatmen'. Its simple melody was already well known to the Russian public, but Chaliapin objected that it was nothing more than a chorus and had only one complete verse which only Russians could appreciate. I said that we would write others and get his friend Koenemann to prepare an appropriate piano accompaniment. This Koenemann was commissioned to do, and he made several attempts before Chaliapin finally accepted the version as it now appears. I was present at the first performance of the song in 1924 and was gratified by the fact that it at once made a hit. From that first post-war concert to the last it always found a place in Chaliapin's programmes, and, if omitted, the gallery would shout until he did sing it!

Almost as famous as Chaliapin's performance of 'The Song of the Volga Boatmen' was his humorous and dramatic rendering of Moussorgsky's 'The Song of the Flea'. In the opera house he was as much renowned for his acting ability as for his magnificent voice, and he is remembered above all for his interpretation of the leading role in Moussorgsky's *Boris Godounov*. Chaliapin's singing, together with Diaghilev's ballet company, awakened the world to the rich traditions of Russian art.

8

MUSIC FOR MANY VOICES

The playing of the merry organ,
Sweet singing in the Choir.

Carol : 'The Holly and the Ivy'

'If we've got to *have* five hundred weighing machines in the
house, I'd just as soon they did sing.'

N. F. Simpson, *One Way Pendulum* (in which the chief
character trains weighing machines to sing the 'Hallelujah
Chorus'), staged 1959

MORLEY : 'IT WAS A LOVER AND HIS LASS'

In Elizabethan times the singing of songs for several voices, with
or without accompaniment, seems to have been a favourite
social pastime. Certainly the habit was well established in 1588
when Nicholas Yonge, a 'singing-man' at St Paul's Cathedral,
first published – under the title *Musica Transalpina* – a collection
of Italian madrigals with the words translated into English. The

madrigal, a form of unaccompanied part-song often on the theme of love, composed for two to six voices, had long been known on the continent. Yonge's collection stimulated a number of composers to produce English madrigals of great beauty, and no doubt other musical households began to emulate Yonge's practice of gathering at home 'a great number of Gentlemen and merchants of good accompt (as well of this realme as of foreign nations) for the exercise of music daily'.

Thomas Morley (1557–c 1603), organist at St Paul's Cathedral and one of the most successful of English madrigal composers, specialised in a subdivision of the species known as the ballett – a song in cheerful rhythmical style often with a 'fa-la' type of chorus: 'It was a Lover and his Lass' was one of Morley's settings of songs by Shakespeare, who was almost certainly a friend of his.

Among other well-known part-songs of the period are 'The Silver Swan' by Orlando Gibbons (1583–1625), 'Sweet Honey-sucking Bees' by John Wilbye (1574–1638) and 'As Vesta was from Latmos Hill descending' by Thomas Weelkes (1575–1623). This last was among the twenty-nine contributions to a famous madrigal collection, edited by Thomas Morley, called *The Triumphs of Oriana* – an offering of praise to the Virgin Queen. Queen Elizabeth was dead by the time the collection was published, but Morley had already had his reward, for in 1598 he was given the monopoly of music-printing in England.

BACH: 'JESU, JOY OF MAN'S DESIRING'

During World War II, a highly successful series of lunch-time concerts at the National Gallery in London was organised by the pianist Dame Myra Hess. She was a fine performer who had a great reputation in her time as an interpreter of Bach's music – though her style would not now be considered authentic – and she was particularly well known to the general public for her piano transcription of 'Jesu, Joy of Man's Desiring'. In its original form, this is a chorale from Bach's Cantata no 147 – an example of a musical tradition far removed from the elegant elaborations of the madrigal.

Taking its origin from the unison plainsong of pre-Reformation times, when congregations had no prescribed part in church singing, the chorale was introduced by Martin Luther (1483–1546) so that all could participate in Protestant services. Luther, an able musician himself, is credited with being the first to ask why the devil should have all the best tunes, and he made it his business to create or adapt simple, stirring melodies for congregational performance. The art of chorale composition and adaptation reached perfection almost exactly two centuries later in the hands of Johann Sebastian Bach (1685–1750). Although he created only about thirty chorale tunes, he re-harmonised four hundred existing chorale melodies and used them to punctuate his great settings of the Passion, as well as his two hundred church cantatas, which were designed to precede the sermon in the Lutheran service.

Bach was also a consummate master of the chorale prelude – a composition for organ based on chorale tunes – and in this he built on the work of such predecessors as Sweelinck (1562–1621), Buxtehude (1637–1707) and Pachelbel (1653–1706).

HANDEL : 'HALLELUJAH CHORUS' (MESSIAH)

Oratorio, like opera, had its beginnings in Italy around the year 1600, and developed thereafter in various ways in different parts of Europe. Handel used the term to describe works on religious themes which in many respects resembled operas and indeed were sometimes staged with costumes and scenery. The church authorities resisted this practice, however, and thus there grew up the tradition of the concert performance of oratorio, with the choir ranged behind a group of soloists in formal dress, and the dramatic elements of the story communicated through words and music alone.

Without doubt the finest as well as the most famous of Handel's oratorios is *Messiah*; though, because of its great double-choruses, *Israel in Egypt* is also rated very highly. Handel composed *Messiah*, to a libretto by Charles Jennens, in the space of twenty-four days in the late summer of 1741. According to Sir Newman Flower's biography, while he was engaged on the work he shut himself up in his house in Brook Street, London, and frequently left untouched the food brought to him by his servant. After the composer had written the 'Hallelujah Chorus' he was found with tears streaming from his eyes; then he said: 'I did think I did see all heaven before me, and the great God himself!'

It was Handel's music which established the great oratorio tradition in Britain; not until Felix Mendelssohn (1809–47) composed *Elijah* for Birmingham in 1846 did *Messiah* have anything like a rival in popular esteem. The solemnities of oratorio suited Victorian taste, and many composers of the period produced them; among the most successful were *The Daughter of Jairus* and *The Crucifixion* by John Stainer (1840–1901). Sir Edward Elgar (1857–1934), notably in *The Dream of Gerontius* (1900), brought renewed distinction to one of the best loved of musical forms.

HAYDN: 'THE HEAVENS ARE TELLING' (THE CREATION)

Joseph Haydn (1732–1809), on hearing Handel's 'Hallellujah Chorus' in Westminster Abbey, is said to have risen to his feet with the crowd and exclaimed, 'He is the master of us all!' (Incidentally, the tradition whereby the audience – or congregation – stands while this great chorus is sung dates back to the first London performance of *Messiah* at Covent Garden Theatre on 23 March 1743; on that occasion King George II decided to stand for 'Hallelujah' and the rest of the assembly naturally followed his example.)

Haydn, prolific in so many fields of composition, was well into his sixties before he composed, in 1798, his first major oratorio *The Creation*. A man of faith throughout his life, he declared: 'Never was I so pious as when I was composing this work; I knelt down daily and prayed God to strengthen me for it.' *The Creation*, with an opening orchestral picture of primeval chaos which was thought very advanced for its day, and many passages, such as the chorus 'The Heavens are Telling' and the soprano solo 'With Verdure Clad', proclaiming the composer's technical mastery as well as his buoyant beliefs, was a great success from the first performance. Three years later, Haydn wrote another choral work, based on James Thomson's poem 'The Seasons'; he called it an oratorio but, in the words of

Dr Percy Scholes, 'its lapses into piety are infrequent'.

Mozart composed no oratorio of note; his mastery of choral composition was, however, displayed in his settings of the Mass, especially the superb Requiem which was his last work.

Beethoven wrote only one oratorio – *The Mount of Olives*, which also contains a 'Hallelujah Chorus' – but he himself rated this below his best work. He shared Haydn's admiration for Handel, whose scores he pointed to on one occasion with the words, 'There lies the truth.'

BEETHOVEN : 'ODE TO JOY' (SYMPHONY NO 9)

Whatever the failings of his single oratorio, Beethoven's skill as a composer of choral music is beyond question. The incomparable choral and orchestral setting of Schiller's 'Ode to Joy' which concludes the Symphony no 9 in D minor (the 'Choral') has become the European anthem, but that is not its only significance for mankind; it is a universal celebration of the human spirit at its noblest. Beethoven also wrote two large-scale settings of the Mass, in C and D major, the latter one of the greatest works of its kind ever composed.

Beethoven may perhaps be held to account for the sheer grandeur of many nineteenth-century compositions. No one went further in this respect than Hector Berlioz (1803–69), whose Requiem of 1837 calls for a huge orchestra and four brass bands plus a choir of, preferably, seven or eight hundred; it is the ecclesiastical answer to Wagnerian opera. Less grandiose but still immensely powerful is Verdi's famous Requiem composed in 1874 to commemorate the Italian writer Alessandro Manzoni; it, too, has been criticised for being too operatic, but such objections vanish before the composer's patent sincerity in one of the most beautiful of all sacred compositions. Brahms also wrote a choral and orchestral work to which he gave the title *A German Requiem*; however, it is not a setting of the Requiem Mass of the Roman Catholic Church but a kind of oratorio – and a very moving one – based on passages from Luther's translation of the Bible.

The Christian religion has inspired some of the finest of all music – and some of the worst. In the Anglican Church a continuing demand for anthems and settings of the morning, evening and communion services has led to much indifferent music being composed for this purpose; on the other hand some fine contributions have been made by a number of able, even great composers.

Thomas Tallis (1510–85) was among the first to set to music parts of the liturgy in English as well as Latin; William Byrd (c 1542–1623), a pupil of Tallis and one of the most gifted of sixteenth-century musicians, wrote magnificent music for the church, as also did Thomas Morley (1557–1603) and Orlando Gibbons (1583–1625). In the seventeenth century Henry Purcell (c 1658–95), educated in the Chapel Royal, was outstanding among many church-music composers.

Remarkable figures in English religious music were a son and grandson of one of the founders of the Methodist movement: Samuel Wesley (1766–1837), who was a magnificent organist, a friend of Mendelssohn and champion of Bach, and Samuel Sebastian Wesley (1810–76), who inherited his father's talent and composed a great deal of fine church music which is still used.

The publication in 1879 of the service-setting known as 'Stanford in B Flat' marked the start of works which were more thoroughly composed and less fragmentary than had often been the case hitherto. Charles Villiers Stanford (1852–1924) was one of a number of first-rate church composers of his time; others included Charles Wood (1866–1926), who wrote a famous setting of 'Hail Gladdening Light', and Edward Bairstow (1874–1946).

GRETCHANINOV : THE CREED

The music of the Eastern Orthodox Church developed in its early stages quite independently of the Catholic Church in Western Europe, and the traditional unaccompanied Byzantine chants, with traces of oriental influence, sound exotic and mysterious to our ears.

From the fifteenth century onwards, new developments took place, particularly in Russian church music; harmony was gradually introduced instead of the old unison chants and, in the eighteenth century, a number of Russian composers trained in the Italian tradition brought a fresh influence to bear on settings of the liturgy. Prominent in this group were Maxim Berezovsky (1745–77) and Dimitri Bortnyansky (1752–1825) who wrote sonorous choral works of great power, interpreted supremely well by the all-male choir of the Court Chapel – the thirty-five 'sovereign's singing clerks' appointed by Tsar Ivan III (1462–1505) had evolved into the established choir of the Court Chapel under Ivan the Terrible (1533–84).

Alexander Gretchaninov, who was born in Moscow in 1864 and died in New York in 1956, was the leading composer of music for the Russian church of his day. After the Revolution he remained in his native land for some time, despite a rising tide of criticism from the authorities for his attachment both to the church and to what was considered a bourgeois style of composition. He left Russia for ever in 1925, and before eventually settling in the United States remained for a time in Paris, where the fine choir of the Metropolitan Orthodox church performed, and recorded, some of his music. In this way Gretchaninov's setting of the Creed, rising by gradual steps to a great climax of devotional passion, became known to the musical public around the world.

JAMES : 'LAND OF MY FATHERS' (HEN WLAD FY NHADAU)

The present-day distinction of Welsh choral singing is closely linked with the role of music in the Nonconformist chapels of the country, but the high reputation of Wales as a land of song goes far back into history. Writing in the year 1188, Giraldus Cambrensis said of the Welsh that 'in their musical concerts they do not sing in unison, like the inhabitants of other countries, but in many different parts, so that in a company of singers, which one very frequently meets with in Wales, you will hear as many different parts and voices as there are performers'.

The words of the national anthem of Wales are by Evan James of Pontypridd and the tune is by James James; 'Land of my Fathers' first appeared in print in 1860 in John Owen's *Gems of Welsh Melody*. To hear it sung by the crowd at a rugby match in which Wales is participating is an unforgettable experience – and a demoralising one for the opposing side. The impression is created that everyone in Wales can sing, and indeed the number of good choirs in the country helps to confirm that impression. Great dedication on the part of the men, and some sacrifice by their wives, is called for in the running of a first-rate Welsh male-voice choir; they rehearse for hours on end, especially when preparing to compete in an Eisteddfod, whether on a local, national or even international level – as at the annual Llangollen Eisteddfod which attracts choirs and other performers from all over the world.

The great Welsh choirs are heard at their best unaccompanied; they can also sound well with organ, orchestral or band accompaniment, but, no doubt for reasons of convenience or economy, they must often make do with a piano. Numerous original compositions and arrangements are available for choir with piano. The two sounds are not, to my mind, compatible, and piano accompaniment spoils many a good choral performance in Wales – and elsewhere, it should be added. For there are other great centres of choral singing in the British Isles, notably in the north of England, in Scotland and in Cornwall; there, as in Wales, the Nonconformist tradition is strong – though singing is just as likely to be heard in the pub late at night as in the Methodist chapel.

SULLIVAN : 'THE LONG DAY CLOSES'

Many of the pieces performed by Welsh and other choirs come into the category of 'part songs', compositions intended for performance by two or more voices to each part; these are less intimate than madrigals, or the glees for male voices which were so popular in the eighteenth century, and slighter both in sentiment and treatment than a full-scale choral work.

Part songs became tremendously popular in Britain and America during the nineteenth century. Sir Arthur Sullivan (1842–1900) was a leading exponent of the form; others were Robert de Pearsall (1795–1856), who wrote 'O who will o'er the Downs so Free?', Sir Hubert Parry (1848–1918) and Sir Edward Elgar (1857–1934).

The Victorian passion for part songs, though it drew on a well-established English tradition, was to some extent imported. Mendelssohn was a frequent and influential visitor to Britain, and his *Songs of the Open Air* of 1839 are compositions of a type in which Schubert excelled. Among Schubert's many beautiful part songs, his setting of the 23rd Psalm is exceptionally appealing.

WALTON : BELSHAZZAR'S FEAST

Of the many fine choral works of the twentieth century, *Belshazzar's Feast* by Sir William Walton (b 1902) is one of the most memorable and familiar. This highly dramatic oratorio for baritone solo, chorus and orchestra is a setting of words arranged by Osbert Sitwell from the Book of Daniel; first performed at the Leeds Festival of 1931, it made an impact which has scarcely lessened with the passage of time.

Two years before *Belshazzar's Feast* came before an astonished public – never had there been so barbaric an oratorio – the International Society for Contemporary Music invited a choir from Czechoslovakia to visit Geneva for the first performance of another highly original choral masterpiece, the *Glagolitic Mass* of Leos Janácek (1854–1928). This unconventional setting draws on a wide range of folk material and treats it in what is often a raw but commanding manner.

Another European choral work of real originality is *Carmina Burana* by the German composer Carl Orff (b 1895); based on uninhibited secular poems written in the Middle Ages by the monks of the monastery of Beuron, it makes an instant appeal through its vigorous approach to melody and rhythm.

Far more profound – indeed one of the most heart-searching works of our generation – is Benjamin Britten's *War Requiem*, composed in 1961. This combines a version of the liturgical Requiem Mass with settings of the war poems of Wilfrid Owen, lending almost unbearable poignancy to the time-honoured rituals of death.

9

OPERA

I have sat through an Italian opera, till, for sheer pain and
inexplicable anguish, I have rushed out into the noisiest
places of the crowded streets, to solace myself with sounds
that I was not obliged to follow.

Charles Lamb

Bed is the poor man's opera.

Italian proverb

HANDEL: 'OMBRA MAI FÙ' (SERSE)

It is characteristic of the operatic ideas of Handel's day that the
leading role in his opera about Xerxes should have been assigned
to a male soprano. The aria 'Ombra mai fù' occurs in the first
act, and is addressed to a tree which affords welcome shade to

the Persian emperor. The melody is universally known as 'Handel's Largo'.

Although George Frideric Handel (1685–1759) inherited certain artificial conventions that were constricting to the opera composer – among them the immense popularity of 'castrati' (male singers whose high voices had been preserved by surgical operation), and the need to provide florid set-pieces for star singers – he was one of the greatest exponents in this field. In recent years, many of his stage works have been rescued from obscurity, thus revealing a hoard of musical treasure.

Since the beginnings of opera, in Italy around the year 1600, its stories had almost all been taken from classical antiquity. Handel followed this practice; his operatic titles, however, were in Italian, since it was the taste for Italian opera in the London of the early eighteenth century that he aimed to satisfy. Among the more outstanding of Handel's many stage works were *Giulio Cesare* (Julius Caesar), of 1724, in which Cleopatra's arias are of exceptional beauty; *Tamerlano* (Tamburlaine), also produced in 1724, which has an unusually dramatic death scene; *Ariodante* and *Alcina*, both staged in 1735; and *Serse* (1738), which was predominately a light and entertaining work.

Outstanding among earlier opera composers are Claudio Monteverdi (1567–1643), whose *Orpheus* (1607) and *The Coronation of Poppaea* (1642) have been revived with great success; and, in England, Henry Purcell (*c* 1659–95), who contributed memorably to numerous stage works. In Purcell's single great opera, *Dido and Aeneas* (*c* 1689), the final lament – 'When I am laid in Earth' – is one of the finest of all operatic arias.

MOZART : 'O ISIS AND OSIRIS' (THE MAGIC FLUTE)

Italian opera still dominated the scene when Wolfgang Amadeus Mozart (1756–91) was born. After writing several early stage works, he produced his first operatic masterpiece, *Idomeneo*, in 1781. Mozart here followed the German composer Gluck (1714–87) in bringing a true dramatic simplicity to opera. Among his greatest successes are *The Marriage of Figaro* (1786), an enchanting comedy with many arias which have become well known; *Don Giovanni* (1787), the composer's reworking, with librettist Lorenzo da Ponte, of the Don Juan story, with its famous 'Catalogue Aria', in which the servant Leporello lists his master's amorous conquests; *Così fan Tutte* (Women are Like That : 1790), an amusing tale of romantic intrigue; and *Die Zauberflöte* (The Magic Flute : 1791), an opera in German with spoken dialogue, a strange, magical blend of myth and panto-mime. Among the best-known passages from *The Magic Flute* are the two brilliant soprano arias for the Queen of the Night, and 'O Isis and Osiris', addressed by the high priest Sarastro to the Ancient Egyptian gods.

Through musical genius and profound human understanding, Mozart transcended the operatic conventions of his time, produc-ing music which illuminated the characters and emotions of the story. He also succeeded in blending the ingredients of 'aria' (formal song) and 'recitative' (linking passages, declaimed music-ally to a sparse accompaniment) into a dramatically cohesive structure.

Ludwig van Beethoven (1770–1827) wrote only one opera, but that a very great one. *Fidelio* is in German, and tells the story of a political prisoner. Carl Maria von Weber (1786–1826) worked devotedly to established a true German opera; *Der Freischütz* (The Free-shooter) of 1821 is a landmark in this respect, while *Euryanthe* (1825) and *Oberon*, written for London in 1826, each contains some fine moments. The overtures of all three operas are often performed, as is the aria 'Ocean, thou mighty Monster' from *Oberon*.

ROSSINI : 'LARGO AL FACTOTUM' (THE BARBER OF SEVILLE)

The Barber of Seville (1816), like Mozart's *The Marriage of Figaro*, was based on a play by the satirical French writer Pierre de Beaumarchais. Both operas are far too good-humoured to echo the quasi-revolutionary aspects of Beaumarchais' work, and the operatic character of Figaro (he is the town barber in Rossini's piece), though irreverent towards his social betters, is amiably so. In the famous 'Factotum's Largo', which accelerates to tongue-twisting speed, Figaro tells how he is rushed off his feet by his demanding clientèle.

While, in Germany, the old operatic conventions were being left behind, Italian opera composers of the early nineteenth century continued to flatter their star singers and please the public with set-pieces designed for 'bravura' display. But Gioacchino Rossini (1792–1868), who excelled for most of his career as a composer of comic operas, was able to use these artificialities to enjoyable effect. *The Barber of Seville*, undoubtedly Rossini's best-known opera, has a number of famous arias, including Rosina's florid 'Una voce poco fa'; and the merits of *The Italian Girl in Algiers* (1813), *La Cenerentola* (Cinderella: 1817) and *Count Ory* (1823) have become evident in recent revivals. Today the musical public has a chance to know more of Rossini's work than a few brilliant overtures and such familiar favourites as the 'Largo al Factotum'.

BELLINI : 'CASTA DIVA' (NORMA)

Two distinguished contemporaries of Rossini were Vincenzo Bellini (1801–35) and Gaetano Donizetti (1797–1848). Bellini was a great master of melody – a quality exemplified in 'Casta Diva' (Chaste Goddess) from the opera *Norma*, one of his finest works, first staged at La Scala, Milan, in 1831. The story concerns a Druid priestess, Norma, at the time of the Roman occupation of Gaul, and this great aria is a prayer for peace. Apart from his melodic gift, Bellini had a talent for musical drama which won him the admiration of Wagner; all his operas, which include *La Sonnambula* (The Sleepwalker) of 1831 and *I Puritani* (The Puritans) of 1835, contain magnificent music of instant appeal.

Had Bellini lived longer, he would no doubt have added to the relatively few – though greatly admired – products now popular with opera lovers. Donizetti, on the other hand, wrote seventy-five works for the stage and only a small number of them are remembered today. Among the best loved of all tenor arias is 'Una Furtiva Lagrima' (A Furtive Tear) from his *L'Elisir d'Amore* (The Elixir of Love) of 1832; coloratura sopranos relish the brilliant display opportunities of the Mad Scene from *Lucia di Lammermoor* (1835). *La fille du Régiment* (The Daughter of the Regiment: 1840) and *Don Pasquale* (1843) are splendid comic operas, while *Anna Bolena* (1830) is, like *Lucia di Lammermoor*, a tragic masterpiece.

This famous declaration that all women are fickle comes from the most fickle of men, the Duke of Mantua, in one of the most popular operas of Giuseppe Verdi (1813–1901). *Rigoletto*, produced in 1851 and usually considered his first mature masterpiece, contains other very familiar passages, such as the aria 'Caro Nome' (Dear Name) and the dramatic quartet.

From Verdi's earlier works, the extract most often performed is probably the chorus of Hebrew exiles 'Va Pensiero . . .' (Fly, Thoughts . . .) from *Nabucco* (Nebuchadnezzar : 1842). When we consider his later works, the profusion of famous operatic scenes is overwhelming. Almost the whole of *La Traviata* and *Il Trovatore*, both produced in 1853, have passed into the popular repertoire. The magnificent *Aida* – commissioned for a new opera house in Cairo and produced in 1871 – contains the tenor aria 'Celeste Aida', and the spectacular 'Ritorna Vincitor' (Return Victorious) for the heroine, as well as the splendid grand march in the Triumph Scene. Great moments also abound in some of Verdi's less frequently performed pieces : *Macbeth* (1847), *Un Ballo in Maschera* (A Masked Ball : 1859), *La Forza del Destino* (The Force of Destiny : 1862) and *Don Carlos* (1867).

The last two operas he wrote are such closely-knit works that extracts are not so easily taken from them. *Otello* (1887), a magnificent musical realisation of Shakespeare's drama, contains 'Iago's Creed' for baritone, and a glorious love duet; but so intricate is the texture of *Falstaff* (1893) that almost the only passage separately performed is a tiny aria for the fat knight himself, in which he recalls how slender he once was: 'Quand'ero paggio' ('When I was page' – to the Duke of Norfolk).

In *Falstaff*, Verdi came near to writing a Wagnerian opera, a music drama of continuous sound and action in which the old formal structure of separate arias, ensembles and choruses has been abandoned. Richard Wagner (1813–83) formulated his ideas of an all-embracing theatrical art gradually; his earlier works contain set-pieces, such as 'Senta's Ballad' in *The Flying Dutchman* (1843) and, in *Tannhäuser* (1845), the Pilgrims' Chorus, Elizabeth's greeting to the Hall of Song ('Dich Teure Halle') and the fine baritone solo 'O Star of Eve'. Another early opera, *Lohengrin* (1850), includes the universally known 'Wedding March', and the exciting Prelude to Act 3, which is often played as a separate concert piece.

Wagner's greatest operas start with *Tristan und Isolde* (1865) from which the Prelude – often said to mark the beginning of modern music – is frequently performed in concert halls, sometimes bracketed with the 'Liebestod' (Love-Death), the tragic final scene where Isolde sings of the union she and Tristan can only find beyond the grave. *Die Meistersinger* (The Mastersingers), produced in 1868, is in many ways Wagner's most congenial work, since it deals with ordinary people in medieval Nuremberg rather than mythical figures. The magnificent overture is often performed; and Walther's 'Prize Song' is as well known as 'O Star of Eve'.

Wagner's supreme achievement was *Der Ring des Nibelungen* (The Ring of the Nibelung), a vast mythological epic which occupied twenty years of his life; it consists of four massive operas: *Das Rheingold* (The Rhine Gold), *Die Walküre* (The Valkyrie), *Siegfried* and *Götterdämmerung* (Twilight of the Gods). *The Ring* was first performed in its entirety in the theatre specially built for Wagner at Bayreuth by King Ludwig of Bavaria. Sir Henry Wood, a great champion of Wagner, used to introduce substantial passages from *The Ring* at his Promenade Concerts – 'bleeding chunks', somebody called them. Nowadays this is less often done, but orchestral episodes such as 'The Ride of the Valkyries,' 'Siegfried's Journey to the Rhine' and 'Forest Murmurs' are sometimes played as concert pieces. Wagner's last opera, the quasi-religious festival drama *Parsifal* (1882), includes the contemplative 'Good Friday Music'.

PUCCINI: 'ONE FINE DAY' (MADAM BUTTERFLY)

The finest operas of Giacomo Puccini (1858–1924) are also

93

compounded of a continuous web of sound, with the orchestra often providing a counterpoint of comment to the stage action. However, in the Italian tradition, Puccini's outstanding melodic gift resulted in vocal writing of exceptional beauty and many individual arias have become popular outside the opera house. In *Madam Butterfly* (1904) the Japanese heroine expresses in 'One Fine Day' ('Un bel dì vedremo . . .') the confident hope that her American sailor husband will return to her; the humming chorus and the love duet are also very familiar.

The first act of *La Bohème* (1896), that masterly tale of life among the Bohemians of Paris, includes 'Che Gelida Manina' (Your Tiny Hand is Frozen), 'Mi Chiamano Mimi' (They call me Mimi) and the love duet, 'O soave Fanciulla' (Lovely Maid in the Moonlight); and in the second act Musetta has her famous 'Waltz Song'. *Tosca* (1900) is a melodramatic tragedy of great power; in 'Vissi d'Arte' (Love and Music, these have I Lived For) Tosca expresses her life's purpose, while Cavaradossi, the principal tenor, sings the well-loved 'Recondita Armonia' (Strange Harmony of Contrasts) and 'E Lucevan le Stelle' (The Stars were Brightly Shining). The one-act comic opera *Gianni Schicchi* (1918) has the frequently sung 'O mio Babbino Caro' (O my Beloved Father). *Turandot*, Puccini's last, unfinished, opera, first performed in 1926, includes 'Nessun Dorma' (None shall Sleep) for the tenor Calaf, while the Chinese Princess Turandot has the thrilling 'In questa Reggia' (In this Kingdom).

The reputation of Puccini's contemporary Ruggiero Leoncavallo (1858–1919) rests largely on the single short opera *Pagliacci* (1892); it brought the composer immediate fame and includes one of the best loved of all tenor arias, 'Vesti le Giubba' (On with the Motley). Pietro Mascagni (1863–1945) is likewise chiefly remembered for one work, *Cavalleria Rusticana* (1890); this is often performed with *Pagliacci* as a double bill.

BIZET: 'THE TOREADOR'S SONG' (CARMEN)

Although Italy and Germany have dominated the operatic scene, France, Spain and Russia each has a tradition in this sphere and, in the twentieth century, Britain too has produced a number of significant works.

In France, starting as court entertainments, opera and ballet – and sometimes combinations of both – flourished in the seventeenth and eighteenth centuries, and Paris became the centre of all that was most spectacular in theatrical productions. The Opéra de Paris, which opened in 1875, has the largest stage in the world, but it was not for this grandiose setting that Georges Bizet (1838–75) composed his masterpiece. *Carmen*, with its spoken dialogue, could not be classed as grand opera; it was first performed at the Opéra-Comique shortly before Bizet's death.

Carmen's immense popularity is well deserved; the story, the characters and the music are all compelling. The score has such well-loved numbers as the exultant 'Toreador's Song', Don José's exquisite 'Flower Song' and the 'Habañera' of Carmen. Although none of Bizet's other operas achieved a comparable success, *Les Pêcheurs de Perles* (The Pearl Fishers) of 1863 is memorable for its much-admired tenor-baritone duet 'Au fond du Temple Saint' (In the Depths of the Holy Temple).

Among the many great names of the French operatic scene is Hector Berlioz (1803–69); partly owing to the immense scale of his stage works, he has only recently received full recognition. Until lately, few people knew much of his massive opera *The Trojans* beyond the famous orchestral 'Royal Hunt and Storm'. Far more popular in the Paris of their day were Charles Gounod (1818–93), whose *Faust* (1859) has rivalled the success of *Carmen* around the world; Jules Massenet (1842–1912), the composer of *Manon* (1884) and *Werther* (1892) as well as *Thaïs* (1894) with its popular 'Meditation', so often played as a violin solo; and Camille Saint-Saëns (1835–1921), whose *Samson and Delilah* (1877) is particularly memorable for the aria 'Mon coeur s'ouvre à ta voix' (Softly Awakes my Heart).

BORODIN: 'POLOVTSIAN DANCES' (PRINCE IGOR)

In the nineteenth century, opera proved a perfect vehicle for the expression of nationalistic feeling, notably in Russia. *Prince Igor* combines patriotism with the oriental brilliance of the Polovtsians; produced in 1890, it was the work of Alexander Borodin (1833–87), brought to completion by Nicolai Rimsky-Korsakov (1844–1908) and Alexander Glazunov (1865–1936).

95

The famous dances are offered by the Polovtsian chief as an entertainment for his royal captive, Prince Igor.

The greatest Russian opera is probably *Boris Godounov* (1874) by Modeste Moussorgsky (1839–81). Rooted in Russian history, it is indicative of the way that music could be used to reinforce the threatened national identity of a country. In 1860, for example, the Czech people of Bohemia won a new constitution from their Austrian masters, and two years later a national opera-house came into existence in Prague. Bedřich Smetana (1824–84) produced a series of operas on Czech themes and in the Czech language, among which the rustic comedy *The Bartered Bride* (1866) has achieved universal success; *Dalibor* (1868), on the other hand, is a national epic on Wagnerian lines.

BRITTEN: 'FOUR SEA INTERLUDES' (PETER GRIMES)

Over the last 150 years opera has changed from being a vehicle for vocal display into a potent medium of expression involving all the theatrical arts – though the changing aims of operatic composition have done nothing to detract from our enjoyment of the masterpieces of days gone by.

In Benjamin Britten (1913–76) England found an opera composer of world importance. As the nature of his stage works does not lend itself to filleting for concert purposes, the four orchestral interludes from *Peter Grimes* (1945) provide a rare opportunity to sample his operatic music outside the opera house. A profound sense of the English tradition can be felt in much of Britten's work; he 'realised' afresh in twentieth-century terms both Purcell's *Dido and Aeneas* and John Gay's *The Beggar's Opera*, and his original operas are often rooted in English history and literature.

Among other twentieth-century British composers who have written operas are Sir William Walton, Sir Arthur Bliss, Ralph Vaughan Williams and Sir Lennox Berkeley. Of all the 'modern' operas in the current repertoire none is more powerful than *Wozzeck* (1925), by the Austrian Alban Berg (1885–1935); brief, and densely packed with musical and human meaning, it must be heard in full or not at all, and flatly refuses to be plundered for 'operatic gems'.

10

OPERETTA

Composers should write tunes that chauffeurs and errand
boys can whistle.

> Sir Thomas Beecham, interviewed in New York, 1961

Nothing is capable of being well set to music that is not
nonsense.

> Joseph Addison, in *The Spectator*, March 1711

The title of this chapter presents a difficulty, for what exactly *is*
operetta? In one sense it simply means a small opera, but it is
generally understood to be an entertainment with music and
spoken dialogue, though the proportions of each vary widely. At
one extreme, operetta borders on opera, at the other it merges
into musical comedy.

The British as a nation do not seem to take kindly to opera –
which is not to deny the existence of numerous opera enthusiasts

and, in the twentieth century, a notable group of British opera composers. In the early eighteenth century, the Italian operas of Handel dominated the musical stage in London for a time, but eventually came a reaction which in 1728 found expression in John Gay's *The Beggar's Opera*. This story of low life among thieves and villains, told in spoken English dialogue interspersed with rhymes set to popular tunes, scored a tremendous hit. It still works well in revivals, and appeals to many people who prefer satire to solemnity and would far rather see Gilbert and Sullivan than *Götterdämmerung*.

GILBERT AND SULLIVAN : 'A WANDERING MINSTREL I'
(THE MIKADO)

Arthur Sullivan (1842–1900) was trained as a boy in the Chapel Royal choir, and in later life was greatly in favour with Queen Victoria. She took a personal interest in his work, and after attending a performance of his cantata *The Golden Legend* at the Royal Albert Hall in 1886 she suggested – as critics and admirers had already done – that he should write a grand opera. Sir Arthur – he was knighted in 1883 – willingly complied with what he took to be a royal command; *Ivanhoe* was produced in 1891, but was not a great success. Whereas Sullivan wished to be remembered as a serious composer, his reputation with the majority of people rests on the operas (they were never called by any less dignified name) that he wrote in collaboration with W. S. Gilbert – though let it be set down clearly that he did write much else besides, a lot of it good.

The string of successes by this famous partnership began with the one-act *Trial by Jury* in 1875; then followed *The Sorcerer* (1877), *HMS Pinafore* (1878), *The Pirates of Penzance* (1879), *Patience* (1881), *Iolanthe* (1882), *Princess Ida* (1884), *The Mikado* (1885), *Ruddigore* (1887), *The Yeomen of the Guard* (1888) and *The Gondoliers* (1889). Thereafter a quarrel about who should pay for a carpet laid in the Savoy Theatre – which Richard D'Oyly Carte had built to house the Savoy Operas – led to a rift in the Gilbert and Sullivan partnership. Their last two operas, *Utopia Ltd* (1893) and *The Grand Duke* (1896), demonstrate that inspiration had by then deserted them.

The story of the relationship between the two men is better than most of Gilbert's plots, for it tells of real people and true feelings; each to some extent resented the importance of the other in the partnership, and Gilbert in particular felt slighted by the lack of public recognition of his share in the work – he had to wait until 1907 for his knighthood. The operas hold the stage remarkably well a century or so after they were written; perhaps they are still best seen in the productions of the D'Oyly Carte Company, which adheres to the traditions laid down by Gilbert himself.

Hopes were entertained that Sir Edward German (1862–1936) – born Edward German Jones – would prove a worthy successor to Sullivan as a composer of light opera; but, although *Merrie England* (1902) and *Tom Jones* (1907) contain much enjoyable music and were popular for a time, the old magic was missing, perhaps for lack of a Gilbert to supply the words. When, in 1909, German and Sir W. S. Gilbert did collaborate in *Fallen Fairies*, the old Savoyard was decidedly past his best.

OFFENBACH : 'CAN-CAN' (ORPHEUS IN THE UNDERWORLD)

The start of the Gilbert and Sullivan partnership can be credited indirectly to Jacques Offenbach; his comic operas had such an overwhelming reception in England that a ready market was created for a home-produced equivalent.

Offenbach, the son of a Jewish cantor called Eberst, took his professional name from the small German town near Frankfurt where he was born in 1819. He settled in Paris as a very young man and worked as a cellist in the theatre before beginning the long series of musical entertainments which made him world-famous. In 1855 he acquired his own theatre, renamed it the 'Bouffes Parisiens', and produced numerous successes, of which *Orpheus in the Underworld* (1858) is the most famous. Like *La Belle Hélène* and other works, *Orpheus* is a skit on the dignified characters of classical mythology; it has been revived with great success in recent years in a number of countries.

The Grand Duchess of Gerolstein (1867) is often named as Offenbach's most satisfactory comic opera, but he himself was convinced, like Sullivan, that his greatest achievement would lie in a serious work. When *The Tales of Hoffman* was produced in 1881, the year after he died, Offenbach's conviction was proved right.

JOHANN STRAUSS: 'ADÈLE'S LAUGHING SONG' (DIE FLEDERMAUS)

After Paris, Vienna was the first European city to be captivated by the charms of Offenbach, for the exuberant frivolity of his approach matched to perfection the lighter side of Viennese taste. Offenbach's work started a vogue for operetta and stimulated Austrian composers to try their hand. First came Franz von Suppé (1819–95); born Francesco Ezechiele Ermenegildo Cavaliere Suppé-Demelli, in what is now Yugoslavia, he was Viennese by adoption. From 1860 onwards he produced over 150 more or less successful operettas, of which we are reminded today by such overtures as *Light Cavalry, Poet and Peasant* and *Morning, Noon and Night in Vienna.*

In the Viennese ballrooms at this time the Strauss family reigned supreme and when, around 1870, the popularity of Offenbach and Suppé began to wane, Johann Strauss II (1825–99) – the 'Waltz King' – was persuaded to turn his attention to the theatre. Strauss had already encountered Offenbach when the Parisian master visited Vienna to supervise a production of his *Orpheus in the Underworld*; on that occasion they engaged in a waltz competition for the Viennese Press Ball. Strauss had no difficulty in winning: his *Abendblätter* (Evening Papers) was distinctly better than Offenbach's *Morgenblätter* (Morning Papers). However, when it came to writing for the stage, it took Strauss some time to find his best form.

Indigo (1871) was the first Strauss operetta; it was a success at the time, thanks to the adulation commanded by the composer, but it was not until 1874 that he produced a real winner in *Die Fledermaus* (The Bat). This tale of romantic intrigue at carnival time has enchanted audiences all over the world for more than a hundred years; the story and the dialogue – by Carl Haffner and Richard Genée – were sufficiently lively to stimulate Strauss, who produced for *Die Fledermaus* some of his best music. Although individual waltzes and other numbers survive from many Strauss operettas, only one – *Der Zigeunerbaron* (The

Gipsy Baron) of 1885 – approached the achievement of *Die Fledermaus.*

Once Vienna's appetite for operetta had been stimulated, it took a small army of composers to satisfy it. Karl Millöcker (1842–99) had a great success with *Der Bettelstudent* (The Beggar Student) of 1882, along with many other pieces; Richard Heuberger (1850–1914) is remembered for the delightful song 'Im Chambre Separée' from *The Opera Ball,* if for nothing else, and Carl Zeller (1842–98) for his 'Nightingale Song' from *Der Vogelhändler* (The Bird-catcher: 1891) and 'Sei Nicht Bös' (Dont be Cross) from *Der Obersteiger* (The Master Miner: 1894).

The greatest master of operetta of the next generation was Franz Lehár (1870–1948). He wrote more than thirty works for the stage, including *The Count of Luxembourg* (1909), *Frederica* (1928) and *The Land of Smiles* (1929), but is chiefly remembered for *The Merry Widow* (1905); this was an immediate, tremendous hit in most of the world's major cities, and still belongs, with *Die Fledermaus,* in the small group of first-rate operettas.

YOUMANS : 'TEA FOR TWO' (NO, NO NANETTE)

Part of the success of the Gilbert and Sullivan operas can be ascribed to their respectability; people were willing to be seen at the Savoy who would have considered the 'burlesques' at the old Gaiety Theatre far too Bohemian. But out of these entertainments, which drew on the broad humour of the music halls and displayed rather more of the female form than was thought proper at that time, there grew a kind of tuneful show which appealed to a very wide public – the musical comedy.

Though it had precursors, the first musical comedy to be recognised as something distinctly new was *In Town,* put on at London's Prince of Wales Theatre by the famous impresario George Edwardes in 1892. The story – about an aristocratic young man-about-town who marries an actress – unconsciously foretold what was often to happen in real life to Edwardes' 'Gaiety Girls', many of whom married into the peerage. A contemporary plot, however fantastic, and elegant modern costumes, were features of *In Town* which set the pattern for successive shows, including *The Shop Girl* (1894), the first of a long series

101

of musical comedies to be staged at the Gaiety Theatre in the Strand. George Edwardes ran both the Gaiety and Daly's Theatre in Leicester Square, where an early hit was *The Geisha* in 1896.

Edwardes soon realised that such entertainments were as likely to succeed in New York as in London, and his major successes were quickly transferred to Broadway. The transatlantic traffic in musical comedies built up in the opposite direction too; in 1898 *The Belle of New York* captivated London theatregoers, who saw it, according to one contemporary account, as 'the brightest, smartest and cleverest entertainment of its kind to be seen in London for a long time'. The George Edwardes style of musical comedy dominated the Edwardian era, though one of the great successes of the period was an independent production, *The Arcadians* by Lionel Monckton, staged at the Shaftesbury Theatre in 1909.

In August 1914 Edwardes, who was taking a cure at Bad Nauheim, was interned by the Germans; though he was repatriated, his health never recovered and, with his death in 1915, a brilliant episode in the musical theatre came to a close. The war years, however, produced several phenomenally successful shows, notably *The Maid of the Mountains*, starring José Collins, which opened at Daly's in 1917 and ran for 1,352 performances; *The Bing Boys are Here* (Alhambra, 1916); and *Chu Chin Chow* (His Majesty's Theatre, 1916), whose record 2,238 performances were not exceeded until 1954 when Julian Slade's *Salad Days* scored 2,283. Since then only *The Sound of Music* (2,386), *Oliver* (2,618) and *Jesus Christ Superstar* (2,620 on 3 October 1978 and still running) have clocked up more.

The musical comedies of the 1920s began to call increasingly upon their leading performers to dance as well as sing. *No, No Nanette,* with music by Vincent Youmans, was a failure in the States but a great hit at London's Palace Theatre in 1925; 'Tea for Two' somehow epitomises the spirit of the decade. Rudolph Friml's *Rose Marie* also came from New York in 1925, ushering in a more elaborate and spectacular series of American musicals, including Jerome Kern's *Show Boat* (1928) and Sigmund Romberg's *New Moon* (1929).

Although the 'wireless' and the 'talkies' might have appeared a threat to the live theatre, the 1930s was to be a vintage period for musical comedy, both in New York and London. The masters of the romantic musical were Noël Coward (1899–1973), with his delightful *Bitter Sweet* (1929) and *Conversation Piece* (1934), and Ivor Novello (1893–1951), whose string of successes began in 1935 with *Glamorous Night* at Drury Lane and continued – through *Careless Rapture*, *The Dancing Years* and *Perchance to Dream*, among others – into the postwar years. Other major productions of the period were Cole Porter's *Nymph Errant* (1933) and the Richard Rodgers and Lorenz Hart show, *On Your Toes* (1937), in which the ballet sequence 'Slaughter on Tenth Avenue' set the style for a new generation of American musicals.

RODGERS : 'OH WHAT A BEAUTIFUL MORNIN' !' (OKLAHOMA !)

Oklahoma! opened in New York in March 1943 and gramophone records of its songs soon found their way across the Atlantic, heralding the arrival of a show which could hardly fail to enliven even the most war-weary spirit. Vigorous and exciting, with music by Richard Rodgers and lyrics by Oscar Hammerstein II, it integrated all the theatrical arts, including ballet, in an entirely new way. It was the start of a postwar procession of dynamic American musicals. Richard Rodgers, a prolific writer of memorable songs, added to his triumphs with *South Pacific* (1949) – in which Ezio Pinza, the operatic bass, had a great personal success in the popular 'Some Enchanted Evening' – *The King and I* (1951) and *The Sound of Music* (1959). Other great hits of those years were Irving Berlin's *Annie Get Your Gun* (1950) and the much-acclaimed *My Fair Lady* (1956) with score by Frederick Loewe.

Two outstanding shows which broke new ground were *West Side Story* (1957), in which choreographer Jerome Robbins and composer Leonard Bernstein collaborated to tell the story of Romeo and Juliet in the context of mid-twentieth-century New York; and *Hair* (1967), with its more experimental and avant-garde approach to the musical.

Among British successes in the 1950s were two small-scale productions with much nostalgic appeal : Julian Slade's long-running *Salad Days* (1954) and Sandy Wilson's *The Boy Friend* (1953), a brilliant pastiche of a typical 1920s musical comedy. Lionel Bart's *Oliver* (1960) was a hit on both sides of the Atlantic, while in more recent times Andrew Lloyd Webber and Tim Rice, with their immensely popular *Jesus Christ Superstar* and – in near-opera form – *Evita*, have put Britain back at the top of the world of musical entertainment.

11

BALLET MUSIC

Dancing, the child of Music and of Love
Sir John Davies, 'Orchestra'

Most ballets would be quite delightful if it were not for the dancing.

M. Bateman, 'This England' column, *New Statesman*

GRÉTRY : 'AIR DE BALLET' (ZÉMIR ET AZOR)

To the Ancient Greeks, the word *mousike* embraced the expressive arts of dancing and poetry, as well as singing and instrumental performances; the 'orchestra' was the space reserved for the dancers in front of the raised stage in the theatres of those times. The form of theatre dance known as ballet originated in the sixteenth century with attempts to revive the relationship between music, poetry and dance as understood in classical Greece; this was part of the renewed interest in pre-Christian

European culture which was such a marked feature of the Renaissance. Formal dances, accompanied by words as well as music, were performed by the nobility at the court of Catherine de Medici in Paris, and King Louis XIV himself took part in the *comédie-ballets* of Molière, among others. With the setting up of the Académie Royale de Musique in 1672, a code of approved steps and movements began to evolve and professional dancers took over from aristocratic amateurs.

A very popular form of entertainment in the French theatres of the seventeenth and early eighteenth centuries was the *opéra-ballet*, a stylised and spectacular combination of singing, acting and dancing. For 150 years thereafter, anyone who composed an opera for Paris was expected to include a ballet, and very irksome the convention sometimes proved.

The Belgian composer André Grétry (1741–1813) produced over sixty operas; from his *Zémir et Azor*, the graceful and haunting 'Air de Ballet' was revived by Sir Thomas Beecham and became one of the most popular of the 'lollipops' with which that great character would reward his public after offering them more challenging musical fare. In 1778 Mozart composed the music for *Les Petits Riens* (Trifles), one of the most successful creations of the French ballet-master Jean-Georges Noverre (1727–1810); there is also a ballet in Mozart's opera *Idomeneo*. Beethoven's music for the ballet *The Creatures of Prometheus*, produced in Vienna in 1801, is a delightful, untroubled product of his genius.

DELIBES : PIZZICATO (SYLVIA)

Sylvia, produced in Paris in 1876, was the last of the three major ballets of the French composer Léo Delibes (1836–91); the others were *La Source* (1866) and *Coppélia* (1870) – a lasting favourite in the ballet repertoire. Though in no way profound, the music for these ballets is delightful throughout. The Pizzicato from *Sylvia* has unfortunately become a hackneyed piece which helped to give ballet music a reputation for pretty triviality; it does, however, ideally match the traditional image of the ballerina, performing on points and wearing the 'tutu'. This style of dancing, with the wearing of blocked ballet shoes and the short frilly-skirted costume, was brought to perfection by Marie Taglioni (1804–84). One of her most notable roles was in *La Sylphide*, a tale of magic and sorcery in Scotland generally considered the first full-scale Romantic ballet. It must not be confused with *Les Sylphides*, choreographed by Michel Fokine in 1907 to the music of Chopin.

Another centre of romantic ballet was Copenhagen where, under Antoine Bournonville (1760–1843) and, more particularly, his son August (1805–79), the graceful style of the Royal Danish Ballet developed. In recent times there has been a revival of interest in Bournonville's works, and the music for some of them – *Flower Festival in Genzano* by Helsted and Paulli, for instance – is quite as pleasing as the well-known scores of Delibes.

TCHAIKOVSKY : WALTZ (SWAN LAKE)

An outstanding figure in the history of ballet was Marius Petipa, who was born in Marseilles in 1818 and died in the Crimea in 1910. After learning his craft in France, to a great extent from his father, he was leading dancer and choreographer in Madrid as well as Paris before going to St Petersburg, where, in 1862, he became First Ballet Master. Of the fifty or so ballets Petipa created or helped to create for the Imperial Theatres of St Petersburg and Moscow, some – such as *Don Quixote*, *La Bayadère* and *Raymonda,* each with an attractive score – have recently been revived with success, but by far the best known are the three for which Tchaikovsky wrote the music.

Tchaikovsky loved ballet and saw no reason why its music should be second-rate; certainly he put some of his own best work into *The Sleeping Beauty* (1890) and *The Nutcracker* (1892). *Swan Lake*, which was a failure at its first appearance in 1877, has – since its revival of 1895 – been among the most popular and successful of all ballets. The choreography of both *The Nutcracker* and the revived *Swan Lake* was shared between Petipa and Lev Ivanov (1834–1901). As stage spectacles the Tchaikovsky ballets are unforgettable, but the music stands on its own, in some ways surpassing in craftsmanship and dramatic passion the composer's purely symphonic works.

In 1890 a young law student called Serge Diaghilev (1872–1929) came to St Petersburg and soon joined a circle of progressive artists, musicians and writers; he was to become perhaps the greatest of all ballet impresarios, and to exert a profound influence on the European artistic scene during the first quarter of the twentieth century.

It all began when he took a production of the opera *Boris Godounov* to Paris in 1908 and returned the following year with a company of the best dancers from St Petersburg and Moscow. For twenty years he ruled over his Ballets Russes, engaging a succession of great dancers, choreographers, painters and composers. He had the vision to encourage the talent of the young; at a concert in St Petersburg in 1909 he heard the short orchestral fantasy *Fireworks* by the twenty-seven-year-old Igor Stravinsky (1882–1971) and at once decided he should write for the ballet. *The Firebird*, produced in Paris in 1910 with choreography by Fokine, was the first of a long succession of major ballet scores by Stravinsky; the music is immediately appealing, in the opulent Russian romantic manner. *Petrouchka* (1911), the story of a puppet at a Russian fair, has a sharper, more brittle quality. *The Rite of Spring* caused a riot at its first performance in 1913, but sounds which were then thought barbarous have now become part of the accepted musical vocabulary. As well as composing the music for several major ballets, Stravinsky also wrote *The Soldier's Tale*, which brings together the arts of dance, drama and story-telling – and he even composed a polka for the elephants of the Ringling Brothers' Circus.

Among other major composers commissioned by Diaghilev were Serge Prokofiev (1891–1953), who became one of the most prolific ballet composers of the twentieth century; Maurice Ravel (1875–1937), who wrote *Daphnis and Chloe* for him in 1912; and Manuel de Falla (1876–1946), whose *The Three-Cornered Hat* brilliantly captured the spirit of Spain in Diaghilev's London season of 1919.

Of all the many arrangements of music not specifically written for the ballet, one of the most outstanding is *Pineapple Poll*, produced at Sadler's Wells Theatre in 1951; for this Charles Mackerras brought together, and rescored brilliantly, a number of tunes by Sir Arthur Sullivan (1842–1900). The libretto, by the choreographer John Cranko, was based on one of the 'Bab ballads' by W. S. Gilbert, and the sets, a Gilbertian projection of Portsmouth, were by Osbert Lancaster. Mackerras devised another successful ballet score – *The Lady and the Fool* (1954) – from the music of Verdi.

Among composers who have arranged their own music specially for the ballet, Sir William Walton comes immediately to mind; he produced a version for full orchestra of numbers from his *Façade* entertainment for the ballet Sir Frederick Ashton created for the Camargo Society in 1931.

There are innumerable examples of works originally designed for the concert platform being used for ballets, with varying degrees of justification and success. While it is true that good music is quite capable of conveying its message without illustration, an imaginative choreographer can create visual images which so perfectly complement the composer's sounds that they become for ever associated with them. One example was Nijinsky's interpretation for Diaghilev of *L'Après-midi d'un Faune* (Afternoon of a Faun) by Claude Debussy (1862–1918); another inspired fusion of music and movement is Sir Frederick Ashton's *Symphonic Variations* (1946) to the music of that name by César Franck (1822–90). The music of Brahms, Schumann, Mahler, Liszt, Bach and many others has been adapted for the ballet theatre – perhaps bringing it to a public that might not otherwise have heard it.

BLISS : CHECKMATE

The great company which, since 1956, has been known to the world as the Royal Ballet, started life in 1931 as the Sadler's Wells Ballet, taking its name from the newly opened theatre in North London. The company's presiding genius then, as for so many years, was Dame Ninette de Valois; it was she who created *Checkmate* (1937) – an ingenius ballet based on a game of chess – in collaboration with Sir Arthur Bliss (1891–1975). His score, which vividly reflects the powerful drama of the ballet, has been frequently performed in a concert version. Bliss wrote two further scores for the Sadler's Wells Ballet: *Miracle in the Gorbals* (1944), with choreography by Robert Helpmann, and *Adam Zero* (1946). Another fine work written for the Sadler's Wells Ballet in its early days was *Job, a Masque for Dancing* (1931), by Ralph Vaughan Williams (1872–1958).

The long list of modern ballets associated with the company since the war includes Prokofiev's *Romeo and Juliet* and *Cinderella*; Benjamin Britten's *Prince of the Pagodas*, staged in 1957 with choreography by John Cranko; and *Song of the Earth* (1966), using the work of that name by Gustav Mahler (1860–1911). Most of the important works in the ballet repertoire have been superbly revived, sometimes with new choreography.

COPLAND : 'HOE DOWN' (RODEO)

The beginnings of ballet in the United States have been traced back to 1735; a succession of European dancers visited the country during the eighteenth and nineteenth centuries, while the companies of Diaghilev and Anna Pavlova enjoyed a great reception in the early years of this century. It was not until the 1930s, however, that American ballet began to acquire its own vigorous identity. *Rodeo* (1942) was in fact written for the Ballets Russes de Monte Carlo, with Agnes de Mille as choreographer, but the score by Aaron Copland (b 1900), rooted entirely in American soil, is typical of the kind of music produced in the United States in the last half-century for dance companies – and for stage and screen musicals, which came to rely heavily on the talents of the ballet world. Other lively ballet scores by Copland are *Billy the Kid* (1938) and *Appalachian Spring*, choreographed by Martha Graham in 1944; one of his most popular orchestral works, *El Salón México*, with its seductive Mexican rhythms, was also used for a ballet.

One important American music-and-dance collaboration has been that between composer Leonard Bernstein and choreographer Jerome Robbins, who were both born in 1918. They produced the ballet *Fancy Free* (1944), about sailors on leave in New York, subsequently the basis of the Broadway musical *On the Town*; and were to work together on other successful shows, including *West Side Story* (1957) with its powerful projection of the dance form.

12

ON THE LIGHTER SIDE

Nº 5. **The Elephant**

Allegretto pomposo

Light Quirks of music, broken and uneven
Make the soul dance upon a jig to heaven.

Alexander Pope, *Moral Essays*

LEOPOLD MOZART : TOY SYMPHONY

From the earliest times, music has cheered as well as elevated
the soul; many composers possessed a sense of humour which
found its way to a greater or lesser extent into their work. The
trouble with humour in music, as in other areas of life, is that it
tends to lose its point with the passage of time. Mozart's so-called
Musical Joke (1787), for example – a skit on clumsy composition
– is no longer very amusing; the loud chord in the slow movement of Haydn's 'Surprise' Symphony (no 94), which may once
have aroused fashionable eighteenth-century patrons from their
slumbers, comes as no surprise to us, and we have to remind
ourselves that the finale of his 'Farewell' Symphony (no 45), in
which the players leave the platform one by one, was intended

as a more or less graceful hint to Prince Esterházy that it was time to give his musicians a holiday.

The most enduring of eighteenth-century musical jokes is undoubtedly the *Toy Symphony* written by Mozart's father, Leopold Mozart (1719–87), and probably arranged by Haydn's younger brother, Michael. Scored for violins, double-bass and keyboard instrument plus toy trumpet, drum, rattle, triangle, 'quail', 'nightingale' and 'cuckoo', it gives young and/or unskilled performers a chance to have a go, and makes an enjoyable party piece for almost any festive occasion.

Malcolm Arnold composed a *Toy Symphony* in 1957, and twenty years later Joseph Horowitz wrote another; this was performed by a group of famous people not primarily known for their talent on quail or cuckoo, and their efforts earned an enthusiastic response from audiences at the Silver Jubilee Concerts at the Royal Opera House, Covent Garden, and St James's Palace in 1977.

BERTHOLD : THE CAT DUET

The 'Duetto Buffo dei Due Gatti' (Comic Duet of the Two Cats) was long thought to be the work of Gioacchino Rossini (1792–1868), but it is now known to have been written by G. Berthold, about 1822, using musical quotations from Rossini's *Otello*. The duet consists of the single word 'Miaouw' repeated with varying degrees of elaboration by two female singers; its mock operatic style is a clever parody of Rossini – who by the age of thirty-seven had written thirty-six operas and in the remaining forty years of his life never wrote another – and also a pointed comment on the nature of the prima donna. An admirable rendering of this duet by Victoria de los Angeles and Elizabeth Schwarzkopf, recorded at the farewell concert for accompanist Gerald Moore at the Royal Festival Hall, has given this piece a new lease of life; it can be heard on HMV record SAN 182.

The solemn absurdities of opera are a perfect target for the satirist, as Sullivan demonstrated, with Gilbert's help, in more than one Savoy opera, and in the comic song 'The Dicky Bird and the Owl', with words by Margaret A. Sinclair. Walt Disney's Clara Cluck was a memorable cartoon coloratura, and the Marx

Brothers made the most of their *Night at the Opera*, while in more recent times Anna Russell, combining comic talent with a good operatic delivery, 'sent up' the solemnities of opera in fine style.

It would be utterly wrong to assume, however, that those who make opera their professional career lack a sense of humour. Enrico Caruso, to take one famous example, was a notorious practical joker; as Rudolph in *La Bohème*, he once sang 'Your Tiny Hand is Frozen' to Dame Nellie Melba's Mimi while trying to pass her a cold sausage.

GOODHART : 'A FAIRY WENT A-MARKETING'

Though composers and musical performers have their fair share of wit, some of them are apparently – and fortunately – unaware of the amusement they provide. We can both smile and admire when listening to records of Dame Clara Butt (1873–1936). The famous contralto was a woman of talent, courage and generosity; well over six feet tall, she had a tremendous voice which could easily fill the Royal Albert Hall – twice, in effect, before the infamous echo was banished – and which carried far and wide across the expanses of London's Hyde Park when she sang 'Land of Hope and Glory' at Empire Day rallies. But when she attempted such delicate trifles as 'A Fairy went a-marketing' the result was unintentionally hilarious. If you listen to this song on an HMV reissue of Clara Butt records (HLM 7025), you will notice how conscientiously she tries to match the coy lyrics with a gossamer-like vocal technique; she succeeds to a remarkable degree, but every now and then, on low notes – in the middle of the fairy tale – out comes the foghorn.

For the most part, however, Dame Clara Butt's interpretive judgement, though outdated, was entirely professional. The same cannot be said of the most notorious warbler ever to record for the gramophone, Florence Foster Jenkins (1868–1964). She was a wealthy American who believed she could sing, and nothing was going to stop her. The climax of her career came a month before her death when she hired Carnegie Hall in New York for a recital of operatic and other arias. It was sold out months in advance, though the majority of the audience came to mock rather than admire. Florence Foster Jenkins was almost always out of tune and out of time, and had no singing voice to start with. Was she aware of the comic effect she produced? It is hard to believe it, but she is said to have remained blissfully unaware. The few records she made have become collector's pieces.

SAINT-SAËNS : THE CARNIVAL OF ANIMALS

Bird and animal imitations go back a very long way in musical history – indeed, music may have begun with them. Few composers have extracted more humour from the animal world than Camille Saint-Saëns (1835–1921); organist, musical academic and prolific composer, he wrote his *Carnival of Animals* for a private performance and would not allow it to be published in full in his lifetime. Perhaps he feared it would damage his reputation as a serious musician, or he may have thought the caustic musical comments in the score, at the expense of popular composers such as Offenbach and Rossini, might give offence. No one, after all, would much enjoy being included among the 'Fossils', though the joke in that section would appear to be mainly on Saint-Saëns himself, since it is his own *Danse Macabre* which is chiefly lampooned.

It is amazing how well *The Carnival of Animals* survives the test of time; such is the resource employed by the composer in his gallery of animal portraits that we can enjoy them over and over again, especially in the original scoring for two pianos and a small group of solo instruments. Nowadays the work is often performed with introductory verses by the American humorist, Ogden Nash; these, however, are rather dated, and there is much to be said for Eleanor Bron's decision to write new ones, which she recites on her record of *The Carnival* with the Vesuvius Ensemble (Bronze BRNA 502).

Surely the most successful of all compositions for narrator and orchestra is Prokofiev's *Peter and the Wolf*; this, too, has an animal theme, with wonderful characterisation of the wolf, the bird, the cat and the duck. Poulenc's *Babar the Elephant* is another such piece, though the orchestration by Jean Françaix blurs the delicate animal effects, which the composer originally conceived for solo piano.

115

Sir William Walton (b 1902) has brought his distinguished touch to bear on most kinds of music, from film scores (including Laurence Olivier's memorable *Henry V*) to symphonies, opera and oratorio. His exciting *Belshazzar's Feast* created a sensation at the Leeds Festival of 1931, shattering all conventional ideas of oratorio. But the public had learned to expect something outrageous from the young man who had composed *Façade* nine years earlier.

Walton, not long down from Oxford, had been staying with the Sitwell family in Chelsea; and it was initially for a private performance that he agreed to collaborate with Edith Sitwell in a quite new kind of entertainment. Some of her poems were to be recited, through a megaphone, to a musical accompaniment created by Walton; since the poems were more concerned with sound and rhythm than with sense, the voice was to act as an additional instrument, speaking the words precisely as prescribed in the musical score. In all, some forty poems were set in this way, of which twenty-one were selected to form *Façade* as it is generally performed, using a reciter, or reciters, with six instrumentalists.

To mark the composer's seventy-fifth birthday in 1977, Oxford University Press published a further eight numbers, under the title *Façade Entertainment II*, which were performed for the first time at a birthday concert for Sir William at the Plaisterer's Hall in the City of London.

Façade is difficult both for players and speakers; it requires great agility and a good feeling for rhythm, and there is also a considerable problem of balance between voice and instruments. Since the original reciters, Edith Sitwell and Constant Lambert, spoke through a megaphone – prompting most of the critics who attended the first public performance at the Aeolian Hall in London in 1923 to declare the whole enterprise raving mad – it now seems quite legitimate to use microphones. In fact the gramophone record rather than the concert hall is perhaps the best medium for *Façade*, since a proper balance can be more carefully achieved and sustained; and several successful recordings have been made of it.

'Listening to *Façade* also presents problems. The words are brilliant, but so is the score, which comments wittily on many popular forms of music; the two ingredients are almost too rich for instant digestion. The music stands well on its own, as is proved by the two orchestral suites arranged from it by the composer.

Today *Façade* strikes us as the epitome of the 1920s – gay, brittle, brilliant, with faint undertones of sadness. It is inimitable; but not far removed from it in style is the *Divertissement* of Jacques Ibert (1890–1962). This is a suite of pieces arranged from Ibert's incidental music to the farcical comedy *The Italian Straw Hat* by Eugène Labiche; like the play, the music is very diverting.

FLANDERS AND SWANN : 'ILL WIND'

Perhaps because it appears to take itself so seriously on the concert platform, 'serious music' has provided clowns and comedians with a perennial source of material. The vast double-bass heaved with difficulty into the circus ring and eventually opened to reveal a diminutive violin; the grand piano which falls apart; the harp whose strings are made of chewing gum – these and countless other tricks have long formed part of the comic routine of circus and music-hall performers. Many of these performers were also accomplished musicians : the late Ted Ray, for instance, whose act 'Fiddling and Fooling' gave so much pleasure a generation ago, and Harpo Marx who, amid the lunatic clowning of every Marx Brothers film, had his solo spot on the harp.

The greatest living musical comedian is probably Victor Borge, the Danish entertainer, whose act is based on a skilful piano technique. Joyce Grenfell, among friends, has a brilliant line of vocal improvisation 'in the style of' various composers and nationalities; her performance, with Joseph Cooper at the piano, is miraculously funny.

The inspired lunacy of Gerard Hoffnung (1925–59), humorist, cartoonist and bass-tuba player, gave rise to the vastly popular 'Hoffnung Concerts', in which eccentric arrangements for improbable instruments offer performers and audience alike the opportunity to let their hair down.

117

Any list of musical entertainers would have to include Donald Swann and Michael Flanders who gave such delight with their two-man shows, starting with *At the Drop of a Hat*. Their animal songs, among them memorable portraits of the gnu, the hippopotamus and the ostrich, brought them particular fame, but they were good at musical satire too; 'A Song of Reproduction', aimed at the lunatic fringe of hi-fi worshippers, still makes its points, and 'Ill Wind', an incessant stream of words set against the finale of Mozart's best-known horn concerto, is a *tour de force* of invention and performance.

13

A PERSONAL TOP TWELVE

'I don't,' she added, 'know anything about music really.
But I know what I like.'

Max Beerbohm, *Zuleika Dobson*

On the BBC's 'Desert Island Discs' programme, the guests choose
eight records to take with them into their supposed lonely exile.
I was one of these castaways in 1968; as long as the raft did not
sink under the extra weight, however, I should prefer to have
twelve, and here they are.

ARR. CANTELOUBE : 'BAILERO' (SONGS OF AUVERGNE)

The makers of Dubonnet proved their good taste when they used
this haunting shepherd song as background music for their
television commercial. I was introduced to it by Winifred
Timmins, known as 'Tim' in the BBC Gramophone Department;
with her encyclopaedic knowledge of recordings she is invaluable
to the programme presenter. 'Tim' steered me towards the most
authentic, and the oldest, record of 'Bailero' – the one made by
Madeleine Grey, friend of Maurice Ravel; fortunately it has
been transferred to an LP (World Records SH 196), together
with other *Songs of Auvergne* arranged in the early 1920s by

Joseph Canteloube. Madeleine Grey's voice has a raw edge to it, and this suits what was originally a folk song of the open air, sung by shepherds as they called to each other from distant hill-tops in the Auvergne region of central France. Many of these songs are extremely appealing, but 'Bailero' has a special magic; it expresses the enchantment of distant places, almost of another world – though very likely the shepherd who first sang it was just feeling cold and lonely and would have preferred to be sitting by the side of a good fire at the village inn.

VERDI : 'RITORNA VINCITOR' (AIDA)

I have an old scrapbook at home which contains pictures and articles about music I cut out of the *Radio Times* in the 1930s; among them is a faded but glamorous photograph of Eva Turner, looking almost like Evelyn Laye, above the billing for a Prom-enade Concert at the Queen's Hall at which she was to sing the Closing Scene from Wagner's *Götterdämmerung*. I don't believe I listened to the concert – my tastes being no more Wagnerian then than they are now – but the image of Eva Turner remained in my mind, identified, quite rightly, with all that was most brilliant in the operatic world. In 1939 I was evacuated with my school to Northampton, and my excitement was indeed great when I learned that my foster-mother's sister, Sheila Wright, actually *knew* Eva Turner, and what is more she fulfilled her promise to obtain a signed photograph for me. Sheila also had most of the records made by Eva Turner, and it was on her wind-up gramophone that I first heard 'Ritorna Vincitor' from Verdi's *Aida*. I was completely enthralled, and although records of this aria have been made by many great artists, Eva Turner's version is the one for me.

In more recent years I have been fortunate to meet Dame Eva, as she now is, on a number of occasions; she has devoted the later part of her life to teaching and adjudicating all round the world, and encourages other artists perhaps more than she knows by her enthusiastic, warm-hearted presence at their performances. As a young woman from Lancashire, she was the first major English prima donna to achieve international stardom on the operatic stage, scoring success at La Scala, Milan, well before

120

she was recognised in her native land. Unfortunately her recordings were few, almost entirely confined to a session in 1928 at the Kingsway Hall in London, when the conductors were Sir Thomas Beecham and Stanford Robinson. The results of that session have been transferred to an LP (HQM 1209); this includes 'Ritorna Vincitor', in which the Ethiopian slave girl Aida, who loves the Egyptian general Amneris, wishes him victory, even though he goes to fight against her own father.

MOZART : CLARINET QUINTET (K 581)

I had rather a difficulty here because I like Mozart's Clarinet Concerto almost, if not quite, as much as the Quintet

There is nothing more likely to turn a composer on than meeting a performer who suggests a whole new range of possibilities for the instrument. Think of the influence of the violinist Joseph Joachim on Brahms, or, in our own country, the case of Benjamin Britten, whose genius responded so readily to – among other sources of inspiration – the playing of the Russian cellist Rostropovich, the voice of Peter Pears or the resourceful talent of percussionist James Blades.

Although Mozart had been attracted by the clarinet since he first heard it in London at the age of eight, it was his friendship with the Austrian clarinettist Anton Stadler, a fellow Freemason, which gave rise to his greatest works for the instrument. Stadler seems to have been a somewhat unstable character who took advantage of Mozart's financial help at a time when he could ill afford to give it; but perhaps the composer was sufficiently rewarded by his friend's virtuosity as a performer and his ability, it was said, 'to make the clarinet sing'. This it is required to do in the Quintet, especially in the slow movement which has an unearthly beauty; it is the kind of Mozartian music which explains Chopin's request: 'Play Mozart in memory of me'. When I first heard the Quintet, the clarinettist was Jack Brymer, so that for me the work has the added attraction of being associated with his congenial personality.

Poor Chopin has suffered more than most composers at the hands of amateur pianists, so I hope no rumour has reached him in the Elysian Fields of my assaults upon his G minor Ballade. This is one of his finest compositions; begun in 1831 under the influence of a revolutionary uprising in his native Poland, it reflects, though indirectly, the sufferings and splendours of that unhappy country. The son of a French father and a Polish mother, Chopin spent much of his life in what he thought of as exile in France; a passionate sympathy with his Polish brothers and sisters, however, found expression in many of his compositions, especially the polonaises and the four ballades. He was the first composer to use the term 'Ballade' to describe an extended piano composition; whether he borrowed it from the *ballades* of French poetry or the heroic world of the traditional English and Scottish ballad – so attractive to artists of the Romantic period – remains uncertain. At all events Chopin's ballades do have a story-telling quality, though only one of them, in F major, has been linked to a definite programme.

The mysterious opening of the G minor Ballade is like the first paragraph of a skilfully told tale, involving us irresistibly in what is to follow: danger, love, battle and triumph – all the ingredients of the heroic ballads of old – connected in Chopin's mind with the struggles of Poland. Indeed one of Chopin's admirers referred to it in a letter as 'the Polish Ballade', as if that was what it was generally called. The immediate inspiration of the music matters less now than it once did; the nobility of this musical saga is universal.

DVOŘÁK: STRING SERENADE IN E MAJOR OP 22

Nowadays there are methods of teaching the violin which can bring a child to concerto standard by the age of five, and the standard of playing among young people generally has risen so dramatically that school orchestras – performing music within their range and under the right conductor – can sound almost professional.

In my young days, our school orchestra consisted of a few violins, a viola, a piano and a cello; with this combination we did dreadful things to the march from Handel's *Scipio* and to Bach's 'Air on the G String', and for some time my idea of a string orchestra was coloured by this toneless recollection. It was perhaps for this reason that I never really took to Holst's *St Paul's Suite*, knowing that it was written for a school orchestra, and Peter Warlock's *Capriol Suite*, skilful though it is, also evoked memories of the scratchy incompetence of our schoolboy efforts. It was not until I first heard Dvořák's Serenade for Strings that I began to take a fresh and appreciative view of the string orchestra.

Dvořák, the son of a village butcher in Bohemia, earned a little money by playing the violin at a time when, in his own words, he 'only just knew that Mozart and Beethoven existed'. Later, having taken up the viola, he played in the newly established National Theatre at Prague. When he came to write the String Serenade in 1875 – he was then thirty-four – he knew a good deal about string playing; he also knew, in his bones, a lot about Bohemian folk music and much of that feeling found its way into his compositions.

The first notes of the opening Moderato movement of the Serenade create an atmosphere of lyrical magic and the other four movements are hardly less attractive, bringing to mind Victor Hely-Hutchinson's statement that 'Dvořák at his best neither thought, nor reasoned, nor wondered, but just knew.' There are several very good recordings of the Serenade, but for my money the Academy of St Martin-in-the-Fields – on Argo ZRG 848 – cannot be bettered.

BRITTEN : YOUNG PERSON'S GUIDE TO THE ORCHESTRA

Some of my happiest broadcasting days were spent as a Third Programme announcer between 1950 and 1953, when my work took me on several occasions to the Aldeburgh Festival. There I met for the first time both Benjamin Britten and Peter Pears, whose work I had first admired through records of Britten's folk song arrangements (particularly 'The Foggy, Foggy Dew' and 'The Ploughboy'). I was able, then and subsequently, to watch

Britten at work in the way he loved best – among his friends, making music at the piano or on the conductor's rostrum in the spirit he also applied to composition – the spirit of a craftsman among fellow craftsmen. This briskly practical streak enabled Britten to work quickly and effectively to a commission, as he did when writing the score for the 1947 film *The Instruments of the Orchestra*, which was designed, like *Peter and the Wolf*, to introduce children to orchestral sounds. Britten chose to create a brilliantly ingenious set of variations on a theme by Purcell – a Rondeau from his incidental music to a play of 1695, *Abdelazar, or the Moor's Revenge*. This work, *The Young Person's Guide to the Orchestra (Variations and Fugue on a Theme of Purcell)* op 34, remains one of Britten's most immediately appealing compositions. If I took it to a desert island with my top twelve it would remind me of the composer himself, of Aldeburgh and of my pleasure in speaking the narrator's part – originally performed by Sir Malcolm Sargent – at concerts with the Royal Liverpool Philharmonic Orchestra, and on a record with Raymond Leppard conducting the New Philharmonia Orchestra (CFP 185).

SCHUBERT : QUINTET IN C MAJOR OP 163 (D 956)

In 1977 I had the honour of introducing, for listeners to BBC Radio 3, the memorial service for Benjamin Britten at Westminster Abbey; in the course of the service the slow movement of Schubert's C major Quintet was played, as the composer had requested, in his memory. I cannot think of a more moving epitaph. The Quintet was composed in the last year (1828) of Schubert's short life and, although there is no reason to suppose he had a presentiment of death, the music is among his most profound, speaking from the depths of one human heart to another.

I first heard it played on a gramophone in a friend's room at Oxford where we were both appearing at the Repertory Theatre at Christmas 1949; it was the old recording made by Isaac Stern, Alexander Schneider and Milton Katims, with Pablo Casals and Paul Tortelier playing the two cellos. The impact it made was so great that I went out and bought it at once.

124

Another memory: on summer holiday afternoons a school friend and I would play tennis on the public courts and then spend an hour or two listening to the gramophone. He had a grand total of twelve 12-in 78 rpm classical records and I had three – the Overture to *Oberon* by Weber, *The Sorcerer's Apprentice* by Dukas and *Finlandia* by Sibelius – and between us we gave elaborately programmed, if repetitive, recitals. One of my friend's records was of the first movement of Elgar's Cello Concerto, with Beatrice Harrison as soloist. This very talented artist became nationally famous in the early days of BBC outside broadcasts, when microphones were placed among the foliage of a Surrey wood to pick up the song of the nightingale; Miss Harrison's solo cello provided an accompaniment and, it was thought, encouraged the birds to sing.

It is hard to believe that Elgar's Cello Concerto is the work of the same man who wrote the *Pomp and Circumstance* marches and the tune of 'Land of Hope and Glory'. During World War I Elgar had occupied himself mainly with patriotic compositions – utterances, as it were, of his public voice; but in 1918, afflicted with the profound weariness of spirit felt by so many towards the end of that terrible war, he began composing the last of his major orchestral works, the Cello Concerto, which was to be heard for the first time in October 1919. From the outset it strikes – or, rather, caresses – a note of elegiac farewell; the work looks back with nostalgia at the world which vanished for ever in August 1914.

BEETHOVEN : SYMPHONY NO 9 IN D MINOR ('CHORAL') OP 125

When World War II was nearly over, a number of young naval officers were invited to volunteer for duties in connection with EVT – Educational and Vocational Training – a scheme designed to equip those about to be demobilised for work in civilian life. By way of preparation for this new task I underwent a short course at the Royal Naval College at Greenwich, and eventually found myself in a Nissen hut on a remote naval air station in Aberdeenshire, dishing out information leaflets to a disappointingly small number of inquirers and supervising the few who cared to embark on training in basketwork or the making of felt puppets – not, it seemed to me, the most helpful preparation for life in the bleak post-war world.

The experience, however, was by no means wasted as far as I was concerned, since it led to several lasting friendships, and Greenwich had offered unexpected cultural benefits, including a full day of lectures on Beethoven's ninth symphony by no less a person than Ralph Vaughan Williams. His insight and enthusiasm were alike extraordinary and, with the help of a set of old 78 records, he held our attention without difficulty throughout the day.

If my collection of gramophone records had to be very limited, I would not wish to be without the life-asserting finale of Beethoven's 'Choral' Symphony, with its thrilling setting of Schiller's 'Ode to Joy'; but I suspect I would want to listen more often to the third, slow movement. This, like the chamber music and sonatas of Beethoven's later period, is deeply spiritual music that brings profound consolation.

TCHAIKOVSKY : SYMPHONY NO 4 IN F MINOR OP 36

Opposite Barratt's shoe factory in Northampton there is, or was, a row of Victorian houses and in one of these I first heard Tchaikovsky's fourth symphony. Youth House, in St Paul's Terrace, had been set up as a youth club by an enterprising master when our school was evacuated in the war. There we held weekly gramophone evenings, based very largely on the record collection of the school secretary, Mrs Rosemary Chirgwin, who was an enthusiast for Romantic music in general and Tchaikovsky in particular. Of course, each side of a record in those days lasted only about four and a half minutes, so gramophone recitals were frequently interrupted while the record was turned over. For those of us who were brought up on these old records, many great works are still inescapably punctuated with 'turn-over points', and so it is, in my case, with Tchaikovsky's Fourth.

It is not surprising that Tchaikovsky's music, full as it is of turbulent emotions, should appeal so strongly to the adolescent – the golden mean holds no attraction for the young. For me, the 'story' of the fourth symphony, confided by the composer to his friend and patroness Nadezhda von Meck – he called it 'our' symphony – was an additional source of fascination : the hammer blows of fate, the artist's illusory dreams of happiness, his ultimate acceptance of the happiness of others, which he can never share. The work might have been designed for a self-conscious sixth-former making his first contact with the Romantic poets and ready to renounce, with Keats, the world

'. . . where youth grows pale and spectre-thin and dies,
Where but to think is to be full of sorrows
And leaden-eyed despairs.'

People told me at the time that I would grow out of all this; I haven't – and I certainly haven't grown out of Tchaikovsky's fourth symphony.

DELIUS : SEA DRIFT

As one for whom words have always had as strong an appeal as music, I find it hard to decide whether it is Walt Whitman's poem 'Out of the cradle endlessly rocking' or Delius's masterly setting of it that chiefly moves me. It is perhaps a case of the perfect match – perfect for me, anyway, liable as I am to be stirred by any good story of the sea.

Frederick Delius, born in Yorkshire of German parents, went to the United States as a young man – he worked as an orange-grower in Florida – and several of his works have American sources of inspiration. Whitman's eloquent poem, about a sea bird on the coast of Alabama which mourns the loss of his mate, suited Delius's impressionistic style to perfection, and this magnificent work for chorus and orchestra brought the composer his first real taste of public success when it was performed at Essen, in Germany, in 1906. It may have been a case of true inspiration, for, as Delius later told his devoted young friend Eric Fenby, 'the shape of it was taken out of my hands, so to speak, as I worked, and was bred easily and effortlessly of . . . the nature and sequence of the particular poetical ideas of Whitman that appealed to me'.

127

Sea Drift is satisfying in its entirety, but it rises to special heights with the lines :

> O rising stars, perhaps the one I want so much
> Will rise with some of you . . .

BRAHMS : VIOLIN CONCERTO IN D MAJOR, OP 77

A love of music is not likely to be nurtured by instructors in naval gunnery, so it was scarcely surprising that the Gunnery Control Officers' course I attended at the Royal Naval Barracks at Devonport in 1944 turned out to be devoid of musical opportunities. However, on Plymouth Hoe there was an enterprising arts centre run by a talented and unconventional army sergeant called Jack Palmer, and there I found congenial company who shared my musical interests.

Committed as I was to Tchaikovsky, I found Brahms relatively tough going at this period, and put up some resistance to the friend who first led me towards the Violin Concerto; nor indeed was I bowled over by its long opening orchestral exposition. It seemed to me then – and I havn't changed my opinion – that Brahms, expected as he was by many people to assume the mantle of Beethoven, felt obliged to produce on occasions a kind of monumental architecture in music which never really suited his genius, and so it is with parts of the Violin Concerto. But in that long orchestral opening is a brief hint of the first movement's contrasting lyrical subject – and when that theme was uttered and developed by the soloist, as I listened to the gramophone that evening on Plymouth Hoe, all my resistance crumbled. To me this is one of the most appealing melodies ever written, and it is for that, and for the wonderful slow movement, that I love the Violin Concerto of Brahms.

It also reminds me of a little incident that occurred at the Royal Albert Hall when we were televising a performance of this concerto with the great Russian violinist David Oistrakh as soloist – an incident which seemed at the time to be symptomatic of the strange new relationship between television and music. Technical matters are naturally of great importance in television work, and, for those involved, are apt to seem more important than the subject matter of the programme. That was the impression I received in my box at the Albert Hall, listening with one ear to Oistrakh's superb playing and with the other, via headphones, to what the TV producer was saying to the cameramen.

As Oistrakh approached the solo cadenza towards the end of the first movement, the producer said: 'Right, Harry, on Camera One . . . come in close . . . that's right, lose the soloist's legs . . . closer still, I just want the fiddle and the hands . . . right, hold it, Harry.' And Harry held it until the end of the long cadenza when the orchestra joined the soloist once again. From the audience there came an almost audible sigh of appreciation for the masterly playing, but all I heard on my headphones was: 'Well done, Harry!'

14

CHOOSING RECORDS

When lovely woman stoops to folly and
Paces about her room again, alone,
She smoothes her hair with automatic hand
And puts a record on the gramophone.

T. S. Eliot, *The Waste Land*

There is now such a vast mass of recorded music available to
the public that the would-be record purchaser has every excuse
for feeling bewildered. Let us suppose you hear a piece of music
on radio or television and decided you would like to have it in
more permanent form either for yourself or a friend – how do
you go on from there?

Your first port of call is likely to be a record shop – preferably
one that takes an interest in your kind of music, bearing in mind
that the classical market forms only 10 per cent of the record
industry.

Apart from the title of the piece, it is particularly useful to
know the name of the composer, because the assistant will almost

certainly refer to a copy of the *Gramophone Catalogue* – published quarterly, and indispensable to all serious record collectors – where available records are listed primarily in the composer index.

You will also have to decide in what form you want your recording -- whether as a gramophone record, a cassette or (less popular in the classical field) a cartridge; the number of tape enthusiasts, and of tape recordings to match their enthusiasm, is growing all the time, and the *Gramophone Catalogue* now has a tape section as well. Whether you settle for a record or a tape, you will now be faced, in the case of a well-known piece, with a number of different recordings : the *Gramophone Catalogue* lists all available versions. If money is no object, you will probably go quite simply for your favourite orchestra, or conductor, or soloist; if economy matters, you will choose a less expensive recording – though this will not necessarily mean an inferior one.

Other questions will also be important. If the piece you like occupies only one side of a record, you will look for something on the other side that also interests you; the *Gramophone Catalogue* helpfully indicates the different couplings obtainable. It may be that the item you want is quite short and is included in a recorded concert or recital with other pieces. In this case, once you have found the name of the piece and the artist you prefer in the list of recordings set down in the composer index, you can look up the details of the particular concert or recital in the artist index; this will tell you what other pieces you'll be getting with the one you specially want.

The thing to do, of course, is to arrive in the record shop fully prepared, not just with the name of the piece and the composer, but with a clear idea of the particular performance you want. Before making a choice of performance, it is a good idea to consult *The Penguin Stereo Record Guide*, edited by Edward Greenfield, Robert Layton and Ivan March; here you will find the best available recordings of a large number of works, classified and compared in readable but scholarly fashion. New records are reviewed at length, and compared with other existing recordings of the same piece, in *The Gramophone* magazine, which is issued monthly; another periodical of great value to the collector is *Hi-Fi News and Record Review*.

The price of records and tapes varies; the most expensive are likely to be recent pressings of top-class artists and of first-rate technical quality, but for rather less money it is often possible to get a reissue of an earlier recording at least equal in artistic merit and fully acceptable in technical quality. Very good new recordings can be found on bargain labels; in this bracket the lower price is made possible by the large potential sales of a popular composition combined with slightly less costly 'names' among its performers.

GUIDE TO RECORD LABELS AND PREFIXES

This brief resumé of some of the major – and some of the smaller – record-producing companies will give you an indication of what to expect from their various series titles, labels and prefixes; though the emphasis here is on records, many companies release cassettes in parallel with new record issues.

EMI

Not unnaturally, there is some competition among leading companies for the title 'Largest Recording Organisation in the World'. EMI (Electrical and Musical Industries Limited) has a strong claim; certainly it embraces the most famous label on any gramophone record – the picture of the mongrel dog, Nipper, peering into an ancient gramophone horn in the hope of hearing 'His Master's Voice'. Great musical names have always featured in the HMV catalogue: Otto Klemperer, Sir Adrian Boult, Sir John Barbirolli, and latterly André Previn and Riccardo Muti, among the conductors; Yehudi Menuhin, Paul Tortelier, Maria Callas, Victoria de los Angeles among many distinguished soloists. Currently EMI is in the process of simplifying the prefixes on its classical labels: ASD numbers are used for full-price new recordings of the highest quality, and SLS for boxed sets of · major works, including some good-quality reissues. In the middle-price range, the HQS label embraces recitals, chamber music and some choral records, while the prefix SXLP covers single records in the 'Concert Classics' series, and SXDW double-folder concert albums. ESD numbers are given to the popularly priced 'Greensleeve' series of familiar classical music, which includes reissues and some new recordings.

An interesting EMI subsidiary is World Records, which operates on two levels. On the one hand, it is a world-wide purveyor – largely by mail order – of boxed collections of middle-of-the-road classics in the 'Gateway to the Classics' series. Secondly, World Records has a catalogue of some 250 LPs consisting of transfers from old 78 rpm records and catering for what might be called the 'nostalgia market'. On these records can be heard once again the great shows of Noël Coward and Ivor Novello; stars of the music hall and musical comedy are recorded for posterity in their most memorable numbers; many outstanding dance bands vividly evoke the social atmosphere of bygone times; and major composers like Constant Lambert and Maurice Ravel can be heard performing their own music, with unique authority.

Also linked with EMI are Music for Pleasure, a bargain-price label devoted to middle-of-the-road and ethnic music; Classics for Pleasure, a very successful classical series produced at a popular price; and Listen for Pleasure, a related label attached to double-album spoken-word cassettes, among them recordings of well-known authors reading their own works.

Decca group

The best-known British rival to EMI in the classical field is the Decca group, with a most distinguished history of achievement since the war. Opera has always been a strong point with Decca, and their complete recording of Wagner's *Ring* – the first commercially recorded set in the world – is an outstanding landmark in gramophone history. Among the famous names chiefly associated with Decca are Kirsten Flagstad, Birgit Nilsson, Joan Sutherland, Sir Clifford Curzon and Vladimir Ashkenazy; the company has had a long connection with the Vienna Philharmonic Orchestra, resulting in, among other things, some very popular records of Viennese light music, and has produced an important series of records devoted to the music of Benjamin Britten.

As with all major companies, the Decca-group records vary widely in price. The prefix SET stands for its top-price classical series, mainly boxed sets of complete operas, oratorios, symphonies etc in new first-class recordings. The SXL series is the main full-price classical label – new recordings of many types of music. In the middle-price range come the JB ('Jubilee') series of reissued classics, planned to form the basis of a representative classical collection; the SDD ('Ace of Diamonds') series of mid-price reissues and new recordings, with the accent increasingly on chamber music, together with the GOS ('Ace of Diamonds') series of mid-price complete opera recordings; the HEAD ('Headline') series of recordings of contemporary music; and the PFS series of popular classics recorded in the spectacular Phase Four stereo system. Bargain-price labels from Decca include the SPA ('World of . . .') series of popular classics, embracing the highly successful collections from 'Your Hundred Best Tunes'; the ECS ('Eclipse') series of classical reissues, some of them stereoised versions of earlier mono recordings; and the DPA series of bargain-price double albums, among them the 'Favourite Composer' series introduced by Joseph Cooper.

The Decca group includes several other important names in the recording business. Argo's main full-price label is the ZRG series which concentrates on chamber-orchestra and choral recordings, and has had an immense success with the Academy of St Martin-in-the-Fields; Argo's mid-price ZK series consists of reissues and some new recordings, notably in the chamber-music field. L'Oiseau-Lyre's full-price series is divided into two sections : DSLO 1 includes mainly chamber music, while the DSLO 500 ('Florilegium') series is devoted to new recordings of mainly early music played on original instruments. The mid-price SOL series from L'Oiseau-Lyre consists chiefly of chamber music, baroque orchestral music and oratorios – a policy echoed in the bargain-priced OLS series of reissued recordings, some of them in re-processed stereo

Another Decca-group label is the bargain-priced Turnabout TVS series drawn from the lists of the American Vox label. This is a mixture of reissues and new recordings, sometimes of interesting out-of-the-way compositions which can be found nowhere else. Finally, from Decca, there is the Telefunken 'Das Alte Werk' series devoted to early music played on original instruments and including many of the works of Bach.

Deutsche Grammophon

On the international scene, Deutsche Grammophon operates under Polydor International, based in Hamburg, but with a number of semi-independent offshoots in major capitals, among them London. In fact the origins of both EMI and Deutsche Grammophon can be traced to the same man – Emil Berliner, who patented his gramophone in 1887 and sent an associate to London to found the Gramophone Company that eventually became EMI.

Deutsche Grammophon has a well-deserved reputation for recordings of superb quality. Among DG artists, Herbert von Karajan with the Berlin Philharmonic Orchestra occupies a place apart; but the company is equally proud, to take but a few examples, of the records already made or projected by Daniel Barenboim with the Chicago Symphony Orchestra and the Paris Orchestra; of Carlo Maria Giulini's multi-award-winning record of Mahler's Ninth with the Chicago Orchestra; of Leonard Bernstein's superb work with the Israel Philharmonic; and of the magnificent complete recording of Schubert's lieder with Dietrich Fischer-Dieskau.

Deutsche Grammophon's full-price yellow label has become a symbol of excellence; the 'Privilege' series is devoted, on the one hand, to medium-priced reissues of stereo recordings and, on the other, to historic mono recordings reissued without stereo re-processing – records, for example, of Beethoven conducted by Furtwängler, and Brahms under Victor de Sabata. The 'Heliodor' red label covers bargain-priced reissues and new stereo recordings of young artists, while the 'Archive' series is, as its name suggests, devoted to early music played on contemporary instruments. Special bargain issues of DG full-price records are often available.

Phonogram

Another great power in the international market is Phonogram, the record branch of the giant Philips Electrical firm; centred in Holland, it has a very important London-based operation. Both the artistic and technical quality of Phonogram records is of a very high order; distinguished conductors like Bernard Haitink and Colin Davis have done brilliant work for them, as have chamber-music groups such as I Musici, the Italian Quartet and the Beaux-Arts Trio, and among Phonogram soloists are pianists Claudio Arrau and Alfred Brendel, singer Jessye Norman, and violinists Henryk Szeryng and Arthur Grumiaux. Phonogram publishes its first-class new full-price recordings on the Philips label; mid-price reissues and some new recordings come under the Festivo (formerly Universo) label; and Fontana is the budget-price label, with an attractive list of popular classics.

CBS and RCA

The two great American recording giants, CBS and RCA, both have UK companies and the rivalry between the two results in a spate of fine and often adventurous records for the discerning collector. The balance of achievement between the two corporations on the recording front has been finely poised ever since Peter Goldmark of CBS invented the long-playing record and RCA first produced the 45 rpm single.

Among leading present-day artists recording for CBS are guitarist John Williams, conductor/composer Pierre Boulez, pianists Rudolph Serkin and Murray Perahia, the acclaimed Juilliard String Quartet and – for lovers of large-scale choral singing – the Mormon Choir from Salt Lake City. While many standard works are recorded in the full-price 'Masterworks' series, CBS takes special pride in such unusual offerings as their complete recording of Handel's opera *Rinaldo*. 'CBS Classics' is a mid-price series of reissues, plus some recent new records by the pianist Fou T'song; the bargain-price 'Embassy Classics' is replacing the 'Harmony' series.

Great artists who record for RCA range from the legendary Enrico Caruso through conductors Serge Koussevitsky and Arturo Toscanini to pianists Vladimir Horowitz and Artur Rubinstein and singers Leontyne Price and Placido Domingo. Flautist-extraordinary James Galway and guitarist Julian Bream are also among RCA's best sellers. The RCA 'Red Seal' label is attached to the company's top-class new recordings; 'Gold Seal' signifies mid-price new recordings and an increasing number of important reissues.

Camden Classics – a company name leased from RCA, whose

136

head office was established in Camden, New Jersey – concentrates on budget reissues and two-record sets of lighter classical material; it now forms part of Pickwick International, which controls 60 per cent of the budget-price market, with the help of such other labels as Hallmark from CBS, Marble Arch from Pye and Contour from Philips.

Smaller companies

Continental Record Distributors (CRD) established themselves as major importers of foreign records – Caprice and Bis from Scandinavia, Pathé Marconi, Musidisc and Ikon. However, the distribution side of the business is now handled by the Selecta division of Decca, while CRD produce records on their own label. Among their best sellers have been Schubert's Quintet in C major played by the Alberni Quartet with Thomas Igloi; ballet music from Covent Garden, including *Elite Syncopations*; Vivaldi's *The Four Seasons* played on contemporary instruments; and Elgar's *Dream of Gerontius* conducted by Sir Alexander Gibson. One interesting recent venture has been the recording of the complete piano works of the Spanish composer Enrique Granados.

The record business has always relied heavily on the creative enthusiasm of individuals – indeed most recording companies, large and small, owe their existence to some gifted enthusiast. The Saga company, to take one example, is the personal creation of Marcel Rodd, who presses some three million discs a year in an old converted chapel in Kensal Rise, north-west London. He loses some of the money he makes by producing a classical list in the '5000' series, which he regards as a personal hobby; it includes many interesting out-of-the-way items which may be unobtainable elsewhere.

Lyrita, founded in 1959 by Richard Itter, has filled many gaps in the recording of British music, issuing works by Stanford, Parry, Ireland, Finzi and Bax, among others; Enigma is a stimulating company formed in 1976 by John Boyden; and Harry Mudd's Abbey Records have, since 1967, concentrated on the English choral tradition. Many other names deserve mention; if you are setting out to form your own record collection, you will, I hope, soon discover them for yourselves.

15

FINDING OUT ABOUT MUSIC

Books give not wisdom where was none before,
But where some is, there reading makes it more.

Sir John Harington, *Epigrams*, 1615

To broaden our appreciation of music we must listen to more
of it more often, experiment in different areas, compare the
unfamiliar experience with what we know already, and be
prepared to amend our views with each fresh discovery, indeed
with each new performance of a familiar favourite. Since music
communicates in its own unique language, there is a limit to
what can usefully be said about it in words. Nevertheless, most
of us enjoy talking about the things that mean a lot to us, and
if music is one of them we shall have endless conversations about
it with our friends – and no doubt indulge, too, in that form
of silent communication which is the reading of books.

The choice, among all that has been written about music, is

vast – ranging from the slender to the encyclopaedic. The standard work of reference by which the rest have to be judged is *Grove's Dictionary of Music and Musicians*. It was first published in the 1870s; the sixth edition, due from Macmillan in 1979, is in ten volumes and will cost some six hundred pounds. Access to Grove is indispensable to the serious student of music, but for occasional reference you can dip into it at the public library.

Of the numerous smaller encyclopaedias, the best and most readable is *The Oxford Companion to Music*, edited by Percy A. Scholes – a huge helping of erudition entertainingly presented in a single large volume. Also admirable, though not quite so useful for instant reference, is the copiously illustrated *Larousse Encyclopaedia of Music*, published by Hamlyn; and the *Collins Encyclopaedia of Music* is well arranged and comprehensive. On a much more compact scale, the Penguin paperback, *A New Dictionary of Music*, is first rate, if rather opinionated. *The Pelican History of Music* offers a reliable and very readable short cut to the historical background of this fascinating subject.

The lives of all the major composers have been chronicled many times over with varying degrees of analytical attention to their music. Probably the best series for the general reader is Dent's *The Master Musicians* which combines a short biography with expert, though not abstruse, commentary on each composer's work; each volume contains a bibliography for those wishing to pursue their study of a particular composer.

In the operatic field, there is nothing to better *Kobbé's Complete Opera Book*, edited by the Earl of Harewood and published by Putnam. Some works now commonly performed were not included in earlier editions, but most of these omissions have been corrected in the 1976 edition. Kobbé, a single large volume, is invaluable for reference but hardly suitable to carry around. For an instant pocket companion *The Concise Oxford Dictionary of Opera* is a wiser choice. Ballet enthusiasts will go for its twin, *The Concise Oxford Dictionary of Ballet*.

Some books about or related to music are very much more enjoyable than others. If you are seeking entertainment as well as information, here are a few suggestions.

The Memoirs of Berlioz give a brilliant account of the sensational ups and downs of a romantic composer's life; among musical letter-writers, Mozart and Mendelssohn are two of the most vivid, and collected editions of their letters have been published; those who enjoy the light music of Vienna will delight in *The Waltz Emperors* by Joseph Wechsberg, and Gilbert and Sullivan addicts will enjoy *Gilbert and Sullivan: Lost Chords and Discords* by Caryl Brahms – both these titles published by Weidenfeld and Nicolson. *Musical Comedy – a Story in Pictures*, by Raymond Mander and Joe Mitchenson (Peter Davies), is excellent. Modern books of musical memoirs include Gerald Moore's amusing account of life as an accompanist, *Am I too Loud?* and its sequel *Farewell Recital* (Hamish Hamilton). Sir Adrian Boult's autobiography *My Own Trumpet* (Hamish Hamilton) is admirable; so is Yehudi Menuhin's *Unfinished Journey* (Macdonald and Jane's). As for musical humour, Victor Borge cannot be bettered: his book *My Favourite Intervals* (Woburn Press) consists of 'Lives of the Musical Giants and other facts you didn't know you'd missed'. And if your musical knowledge isn't all it might be – and whose is? – look out for the Bluffer's Guides (Wolfe Publishing Ltd) and let Peter Gammond tell you how to *Bluff Your Way in Music*.

Of musical periodicals, probably the most useful for the general listener is *Music and Musicians*, published monthly by Hansom Books, PO Box 294, 2 and 4 Old Pye Street, off Strutton Ground, London SW1P 2LR. As mentioned in the previous chapter, *The Gramophone* and *Hi-Fi News*, both available from newsagents, give useful information on the choice of records. *Radio Times* and *The Listener* often include contributions of musical interest (BBC Publications also produce the modestly priced and well produced BBC Music Guides on various aspects of the subject); and musical events are of course discussed at length in the more serious daily and Sunday newspapers.

Advertisements of forthcoming musical performances also appear in the papers, but a speedier and more reliable way of obtaining advance information is to join the mailing lists operated by most musical organisations. This usually involves a small subscription. For example, £1.50 a year (1978 price) will bring you information about all concerts and other events on London's

South Bank: write to the Mailing Department, Royal Festival Hall, South Bank, London SE1 8XX. The Royal Opera House, Covent Garden and the English National Opera at the London Coliseum have a joint mailing list which at the time of writing costs £1.25 a year; for this amount subscribers get full advance details of all performances at both theatres and occasional special offers. Applicants should write to the Mailing List Department at the London Coliseum, St Martin's Lane, London WC2N 4ES.

The programme for the annual two-month season of Henry Wood Promenade Concerts is published well in advance by BBC Publications at 35 Marylebone High Street, London W1M 4AA, and can be obtained from the Royal Albert Hall and from many newsagents and booksellers. Postal booking for all concerts normally opens about a month before the start of the season at the Box Office, Royal Albert Hall, London SW7 2AP, and at the other locations in London where Proms are now held; season tickets can be obtained by post only from the Royal Albert Hall after the advertised date of the start of postal booking. A season ticket will include admission to the Last Night of the season; otherwise those wishing to attend this extremely popular occasion must apply to be included in a ballot for tickets. To do this, write to the Royal Albert Hall Box Office not later than 27 May; you should enclose your address, but there is no need to send a stamp for return postage.

Arrangements similar to those for musical events in London are made in other musical centres throughout the country, and for the many festivals held each year. Advance information can always be obtained from the relevant office; in many cases there are concessions for parties, and above all for the young. These vary from place to place, and the best advice to those under twenty-five is to join 'Youth and Music', a national organisation dedicated to providing young people with cheap access to good music. A free leaflet explaining how Youth and Music works – and how to get reductions of up to 50 per cent on seat prices – is available from their London office at 40, William IV Street, London WC2.

141

INDEX

143